Christmas is Coming!
1989

Compiled and Edited
by Linda Martin Stewart

Oxmoor House®

Library of Congress Catalog Card Number: 84-63030
ISBN: 0-8487-0745-1
ISSN: 0883-9077
Manufactured in the United States of America
First Printing

Executive Editor: Nancy J. Fitzpatrick
Production Manager: Jerry Higdon
Associate Production Manager: Rick Litton
Art Director: Bob Nance

Christmas Is Coming! 1989

Editor: Linda Martin Stewart
Illustrator and Designer: Barbara Ball
Editorial Assistants: Laura Miller Kurtz,
  Alice London Cox
Production Assistant: Theresa L. Beste
Copy Chief: Mary Jean Haddin
Photographer: Colleen Duffley
Photo Stylist: Connie Formby

To find out how you can order *Cooking Light*
magazine, write to *Cooking Light*®, P.O. Box
C-549, Birmingham, AL 35283

Contents

Dear Kids.................................4

A Word to Parents................ 5

Christmas Around the World

New Faces and Friends......................8
Christmas Gift-Givers.................... 10
Nisse Dolls.................................... 11
St. Lucia's Day................................ 12
Las Posadas.................................. 12
Let's Make a Piñata........................ 13
Away in a Manger.......................... 14
The First Christmas Tree................ 15
A Friendship Star........................... 15
Christmas in Australia.................... 16
Christmas in Our Newest States......17
Merry Christmas to All................... 18

**Juan and
Lucila Cueva
Peru**

Children's Workshop: Happy Holiday Crafts

Trimmings to Fix

Peppermint Ponies.....................22
Cookie-Cutter Kids.........................24
Santa Cones....................................26
Jumping Jack.................................28
Cheery Trio...................................30
Paper Plate Angel.........................33
Shoe-Box Train.............................36
Window Wonderland......................38
A Colorful Crèche......................... 40
Handy-Dandy Door Decoration.......44
Sponge Wrap................................46
Reindeer Wrap..............................48
Patchwork Cards...........................51

Presents to Make

Cowboy Pete........................ 54
Santa Claus Paperdolls... 57
Nifty Necklaces........... 62
Hand-Painted
   Potholders.............. 64
Stenciled Garden
   Gear..................... 66
Pet Stockings............ 68

Parents' Workshop: Great Gifts for Children

Grin and Wear It

Chris-Mouse Sleep Set.................... 74
Cow Sweater................................... 77
Blue-Ribbon Bibs............................80
Pocket Pony Sweatsuit....................86
Buttons 'n Bows............................. 90
Vest-Dressed.................................92

Just for Fun

Santa Puzzle................................... 98
Sugarplum Fairy Wand................. 100
Goodnight, Barrettes..................... 103
Kangaroo Camp Kit.......................106
Teddy Peg Rack............................112
Honey Bunny................................ 116
Crocodile Crunch........................ 120
Dear Dolly Hangers...................... 124
Wooden Plane.............................. 126
Missy Mouse Pajama Bag.............. 130
Jungle Tent..................................136

Designers & Contributors

Designers & Contributors......................... 144

Dear Kids

Did you ever wonder how children in other countries celebrate Christmas? In our new section, "Christmas Around the World," you'll meet boys and girls from many lands and find out how their Christmas customs differ from ours. You'll read about the first crèche and the first Christmas tree. And you'll learn how to make *nisse* (Norwegian gnome) dolls, a Mexican *piñata,* and a special paper friendship star.

The next stop is "Children's Workshop." Here you'll find decorations for sprucing up your tree, your house—even your classroom door! There are instructions for sponge-painting wrapping paper and for piecing patchwork cards. As for gifts to make, there's a Cowboy Pete pencil holder, Santa Claus Paperdolls, Hand-Painted Mitts—and more!

Before you begin a project, check with a grown-up to make sure it's a suitable one for you to make. The projects labeled Level 1 are the easiest. Level 2 projects are simple, too, but take longer to complete. The most difficult projects are labeled Level 3.

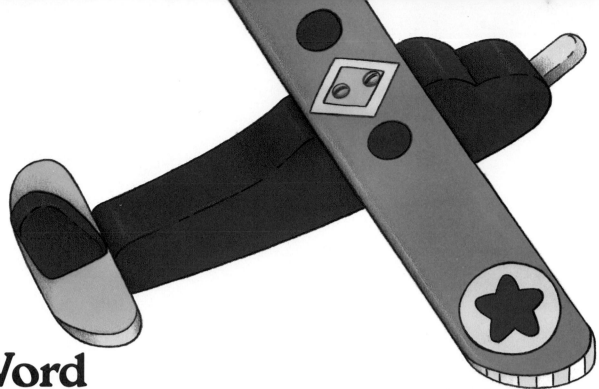

A Word to Parents

Because this book is created for children, it makes sense to fill its pages with cute kids and crayon-bright color. And thanks to an imaginative trio—Connie, Colleen, and Barbara—*CHRISTMAS IS COMING! 1989* is bursting at the binding with both.

As photo stylist extraordinaire, Connie Formby rounds up the models and their wardrobes and myriad props for the photographs in *CHRISTMAS IS COMING!* While Connie dresses the children and puts the finishing touches on her remarkable foam-core creations (for example, the cow on page 77), photographer Colleen Duffley sets up her lights and camera and readies everyone for action. A natural with kids—and adults, too, for that matter—Colleen has an easygoing playfulness that brings out the best in her subjects.

With photographs in hand, Barbara Ball sets about her task of designing and illustrating *CHRISTMAS IS COMING!* A bundle of talent, Barbara has an uncanny ability to look at the children's projects, read the instructions, and zero in on the steps that need illustrations. This, combined with her flair for drawing and eye for color, makes Barbara invaluable for the job.

As always you and your children will find plenty to keep you busy with the projects proffered in *CHRISTMAS IS COMING!* Before you start making your holiday gifts, however, sit down with your youngsters and read through this year's special chapter, "Christmas Around the World." It's guaranteed to be a seasonal treat.

Happy holidays!

Linda Martin Stewart

Christmas Around the World

New Faces and Friends

Christmas! What an exciting time of year for boys and girls—and grown-ups, too. There's a cheerful spirit in the air. Feelings of love and goodwill fill our hearts. We smile readily and are thoughtful of others.

The weeks before Christmas are busy ones. Families shop for presents, bake cookies, and search for the perfect Christmas tree. Dad checks the lights, and Mom unpacks the ornaments that have been carefully stored away. The tree goes up, the stockings are hung, and the wait for Santa begins!

As most of you know, Jesus' birthday was the very first Christmas. All over the world, people celebrate this special holiday. Many of these people live in faraway lands, and many have customs and traditions that are very different from ours.

Learning about these customs and traditions is lots of fun. Let's begin by meeting some kids from other countries and checking the map to see where they live.

ARCTIC OCEAN

Canada

Kathryn and Robert McClelland are from Canada. On Christmas Day, it is very cold, and there is plenty of snow. After opening presents, Kathryn and Robert bundle up. They go outside to ski, ice-skate, and race downhill on their toboggans.

NORTH AMERICA

PACIFIC OCEAN

Venezuela

SOUTH AMERICA

Adriana Christina and Carolina Ugueto are cousins. In their native country, Venezuela, Christmas Eve is called *Noche Buena,* which means the Good Night. It is a time for feasting and dancing. At midnight, they go to church. When at last they go to sleep, the Baby Jesus brings them presents.

ANTARCTICA

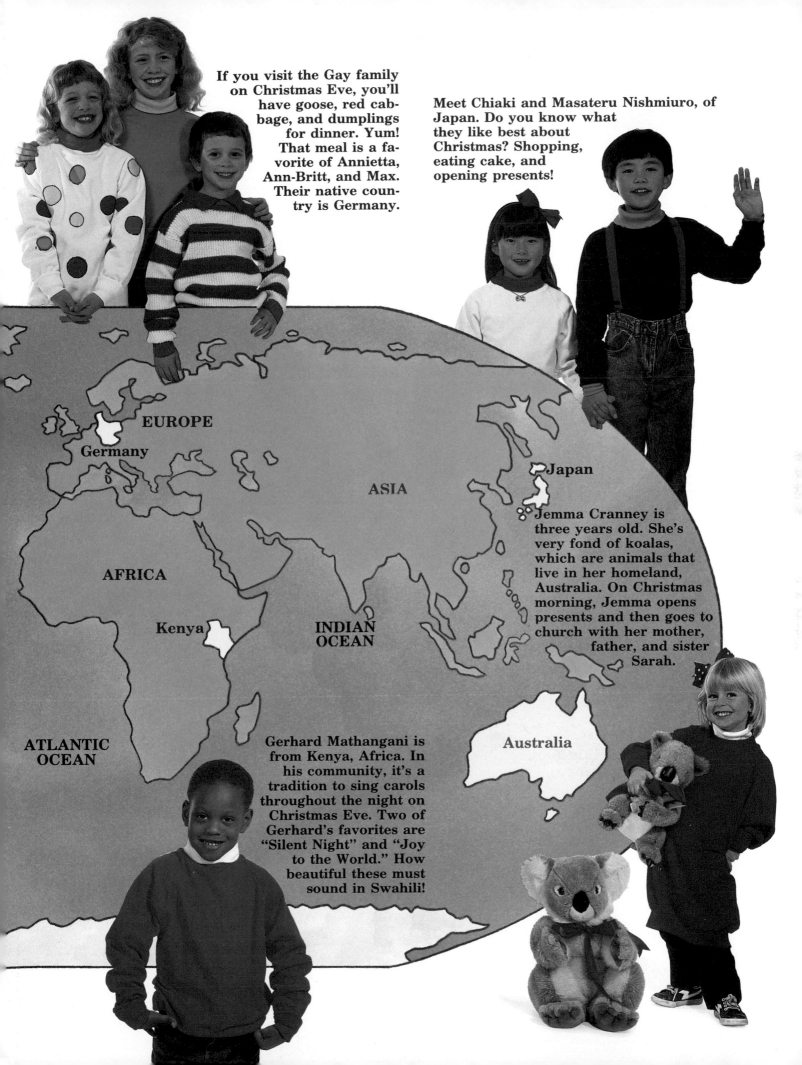

If you visit the Gay family on Christmas Eve, you'll have goose, red cabbage, and dumplings for dinner. Yum! That meal is a favorite of Annietta, Ann-Britt, and Max. Their native country is Germany.

Meet Chiaki and Masateru Nishmiuro, of Japan. Do you know what they like best about Christmas? Shopping, eating cake, and opening presents!

EUROPE

Germany

ASIA

Japan

AFRICA

Kenya

INDIAN OCEAN

Jemma Cranney is three years old. She's very fond of koalas, which are animals that live in her homeland, Australia. On Christmas morning, Jemma opens presents and then goes to church with her mother, father, and sister Sarah.

ATLANTIC OCEAN

Australia

Gerhard Mathangani is from Kenya, Africa. In his community, it's a tradition to sing carols throughout the night on Christmas Eve. Two of Gerhard's favorites are "Silent Night" and "Joy to the World." How beautiful these must sound in Swahili!

Viejito Pascuero
by Georgette Palominos
age 7
Santiago, Chile

Christmas Gift-Givers

In America, it's a jolly old man named Santa Claus who fills our stockings and leaves us presents on Christmas Eve. Although we never see Santa at work (for he'll only come if we're asleep), we know that he wears a bright red suit and that he travels through the air in a reindeer-drawn sleigh. We know also that he's fond of cookies and milk, and good little girls and boys.

The first Christmas gift-givers were the Magi, or Wise Men. Twelve days after Jesus was born, the Wise Men brought him gold and incense. In Spain and Portugal, on January 5th, children set out their empty shoes for the Wise Men to fill. For the camels, which must get very weary, the children leave water and bundles of straw.

On January 6th, children in Italy also find their gifts. There, it's a kind witch who fills the shoes that have been left by the fireplace. Her name is *Befana*. Legend says that the Wise Men invited Befana to go with them to Bethlehem, but she was too busy sweeping her floor. Now, at Christmas, she flies on her broom, looking for Bethlehem and leaving gifts for children along the way.

In Switzerland, a child angel delivers the gifts. Dressed in white and wearing a veil and jeweled crown, *Christkindli* arrives in a sleigh. Other children dressed in white accompany him. They sing carols as the angel goes from house to house, handing out gifts and Christmas trees.

Gift-givers in Norway and Denmark are gnomes. They are called *Jule-Nisser*. Like Santa, the nisser wear red hats and have long white whiskers. However, they are very tiny—so tiny, in fact, that one can live in a crack in a door! The nisser guard the farm animals and make sure that the house is clean for Christmas. As a reward, children leave the gnomes bowls of rice pudding, which is their favorite dessert. In return, the nisser leave presents.

Père Noël
by Yan Sanchez
age 8
Paris, France

In England, Santa is known as Father Christmas. The French call him *Père Noël*. Saint Nicholas, or *Sinterklaas*, delivers gifts to kids in Holland.

10

Nisse Dolls

These gnomes look merry sitting on a table, tied onto presents, or hanging on the tree.

To make the dolls, you'll need yarn, a 6″ square of cardboard, scissors, a ruler, a pencil, tracing paper, red and white felt, and white glue.

For each nisse (that's singular for nisser), wrap a piece of yarn around the cardboard 31 times. At one end of the cardboard, slip a piece of yarn around the loops and tie it tightly. Cut the loops at the other end and remove the cardboard. Cut six more pieces of yarn, to tie off sections of the doll.

Tie off the head 1½″ from the looped end. For each arm, pull away 12 strands of yarn and tie them off 2½″ from the ends. Tie off the waist 1½″ from the head. For legs, divide the rest of the strands in half and tie them off near the ends.

Trim the ties. Below the ties, trim the arms to shorten them and trim the legs to make them even.

Trace the patterns and cut them out. Cut one beard and one hat from felt. Glue the beard in place. With the hat, make a cone to fit the doll's head. Glue the hat to the head, covering the ends of the beard. Let dry.

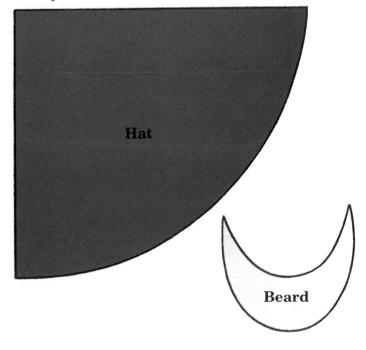

Hat

Beard

11

St. Lucia's Day

In Sweden, Christmas lasts for a whole month. It begins on December 13, which is known as St. Lucia's Day.

Lucia was born about 300 years after Jesus, on the island of Sicily. At that time, most people in Sicily were pagans. They worshipped idols. Lucia was a Christian, and she told people about Jesus. When she wouldn't marry a pagan suitor, Lucia was killed.

Many years later, missionaries carried this story to Sweden. Today, Sweden honors St. Lucia in a very special way.

Early on the morning of December 13, a young girl in each home awakens the family with coffee and freshly baked buns. Dressed as the Bride Lucia, she wears a white dress and red sash. On her head is a wreath of seven lighted candles. These candles are symbols of light, which is the meaning of the name Lucia.

Other children in the family often accompany the Bride Lucia. Dressed in white robes and tall, pointed hats, Lucia's brothers carry star wands and are known as Star Boys. Lucia's sisters wear white also, but instead of candles, they wear glitter in their hair.

Las Posadas

In Mexico, the main celebration at Christmas is Las Posadas. *Posada* is the Spanish word for inn. For nine nights, families and friends go from house to house, just as Mary and Joseph went from inn to inn, looking for hospitality. There are Christmas prayers and songs. Afterwards, there's a *piñata* party.

A piñata is a clay jar that has been filled with candy and tiny toys and then decorated with brightly colored paper. It

Malin and Rikard Jonsson celebrate St. Lucia's Day. This year, Malin was the Bride Lucia. Next year, her twin sister, Maria, will have that honor.

is hung outdoors from the branch of a tree. One after another, the children at the party are blindfolded. They are given a long stick and three chances to break the piñata. Whack! At last someone succeeds. What a scramble there is for the treats that fall to the ground!

Let's Make a Piñata

Piñatas come in all shapes and sizes. Some look like fish. Others look like birds or animals. Here's how to make a papier-mâché one that looks like a star.

You'll need measuring cups, white glue (water-soluble), an old pan and spoon, newspapers, an inflated balloon, 13 cone-shaped paper cups, masking tape, ½″-diameter rope, scissors, two rolls of 1¾″-wide crepe paper (one orange and one yellow), and treats.

Mix ½ cup of glue with ⅛ cup of water in the pan. (Mix more glue as you need it.) Tear the newspaper into ½″ x 4″ strips and dip them in the glue mixture. Cover all of the balloon, except a 1½″ circle at the tied end and a ½″ circle at the opposite end, with strips. Let dry. Repeat two times.

Turn the balloon so that the 1½″ bare spot is at the top. Tape 12 of the cups to the balloon, saving the last cup for later. (Do not cover the bare spots with cups.) Secure the cups with glue-dipped strips.

Walter Saenz takes a whack at the star piñata!

When the strips are dry, pop the balloon. Run the rope through the holes and knot it at the bottom hole. Fill the hollow with treats. Cut the tip off the last cup. Poke the rope at the top of the piñata through the hole in the cup. Secure the cup to the piñata with glue-dipped strips. Let dry.

Cut thirteen 8″-long strips of orange crepe paper. Cut slits to fringe one long edge of each strip. Put glue on the ends of the strips. Wrap the strips around the tips of the cups. Cover the rest of the piñata with fringed strips of yellow crepe paper. Let the glue dry.

Away in a Manger

St. Francis was a monk who lived in Assisi, Italy, many centuries ago. At Christmas, St. Francis would tell the story of Jesus' birth to the villagers at church. How he hoped to open their hearts to the glory of Christmas! But each year, the service would end, and St. Francis would feel that he had failed.

One Christmas, as he was walking to church, St. Francis saw some men tending their sheep in the fields. The men were huddled around fires, and they reminded St. Francis of the shepherds who were keeping watch over their flocks the night that Jesus was born. The sight stirred the monk's heart, and he wondered then if seeing the Nativity would bring it to life for the villagers.

That Christmas, St. Francis set up a manger filled with straw and a waxen figure of the Baby Jesus. Around the manger stood live oxen and sheep—and real people dressed as Mary and Joseph, the shepherds, and the kings. What a glorious sight it must have been!

Today, there's a miniature manger scene in almost every home in Italy. There the Nativity is called *presepe,* which means stable. In France, the scene is called *crèche,* or cradle, and in Germany, it is called *krippe,* or crib.

14

El Pesebre
by Ana Maria Bresciani
age 10
Bogotá, Colombia

The First Christmas Tree

Long ago, on a snowy night in Germany, a man named Martin Luther was walking through the forest. It was December, and Mr. Luther's thoughts were on Christmas. As he looked up at the sky, the stars seemed to be twinkling on the branches of the trees. How lovely it would be, he thought, to have a tree indoors for Christmas. So he cut a small fir, took it home, and decorated it with candles. When they were lit, the flames flickered. "Oh," his family cried, "the lights look just like twinkling stars!"

A Friendship Star

Have you ever cut snowflakes from folded tissue paper? Making this decoration is similar to that, but twice the fun. (You get to color it!)

You'll need a 10″ x 10″ piece of white paper (light to medium weight), a ruler and pencil, a small pair of sharp scissors, and colored markers.

Fold the piece of paper in half. Fold the paper in half again. Turn the paper so that the unfolded corner is at the top, on the left-hand side.

On the top and left-hand edges of the paper, make a mark 2⅛″ from the unfolded corner. Draw lines, very lightly, from the 2⅛″ marks to the corner opposite the unfolded corner. These lines will divide the paper into thirds.

Fold the first third toward the front and over the center third. Fold the last third toward the back and over the center third.

Trace the pattern and cut it out. Draw around the pattern (solid lines only) on the folded paper. Cut out the friendship star, cutting only on the solid lines. Unfold the star and color it.

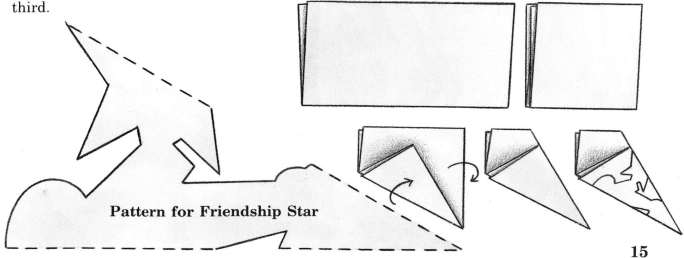

Pattern for Friendship Star

Christmas in Australia

Australia is the world's largest island and smallest continent. The land there is flat, dry, and very old. The country, however, is new. Like America, Australia was first settled by families from England.

Australia lies in the southern hemisphere, which means the seasons there are the opposite of ours. When Christmas comes to Australia, it is summertime and very hot. Father Christmas (good sport that he is) ignores the heat and delivers gifts in Australia on Christmas Eve, just as he does in England.

In addition to the arrival of Father Christmas, "Carols by Candlelight" is an exciting event on Christmas Eve. All over the country, thousands of people gather in the city parks and sing carols while holding lit candles. How joyful those songs must sound!

On Christmas morning, families open their gifts at the breakfast table and, afterwards, go to church. When they come home, they have roast turkey and plum pudding for dinner, just like their English ancestors. On Christmas afternoon, however, the Australians have a tradition that the English don't share. They put on their swimsuits, pack a picnic supper, and head for some fun in the sun at the beach!

Christmas Day in Australia is a summer sizzler!

16

Christmas in Our Newest States

When Santa lands in Alaska, he's probably quite thankful for his thick beard and warm woolen suit. Winters there are bitter cold, and much of the land is covered with ice and snow. Outdoor activities include ice fishing and sled dog racing. Brrr. . . .

Alaska became our 49th state in 1959. Since then, many Alaskans have adopted American customs and traditions. At Christmas, families decorate trees, hang up stockings, and enjoy a big dinner.

One native custom that Alaskans celebrate is called "starring." A large star is made with colored paper and tinsel and mounted on a pole. As a chosen leader carries the star from house to house, the rest of the children and grown-ups follow, acting as the Wise Men who followed the star to Bethlehem. The group carry lanterns and sing carols as they go. Often they're invited inside to get warm and have refreshments.

Our 50th state, Hawaii, is a popular place to vacation. Rather than being a chunk of land like our other states, Hawaii is a chain of islands. There, the skies are sunny and blue throughout most of the year. Because of all the water and the balmy weather, Hawaiians claim that when Santa comes to their state, he sets his sleigh aside and travels by boat.

At Christmas, Hawaiian children enjoy a two-week vacation from school, just like other American kids. At night, they sing carols to the music of guitars and ukuleles. *Mele Kalikimaka,*" they shout, wishing one another a "Merry Christmas."

There are lots of palm and coconut trees in Hawaii but very few evergreens. This means that Christmas trees must be brought in from the mainland (the continental United States). Most of these trees come from Oregon and Washington, and they arrive by ship.

Christmas trees are very popular in Hawaii, and in December, there is one in almost every home and schoolroom. Some of the islanders spray their trees white, to make them look snowy. Hawaiians decorate their trees beautifully, not only with balls and tinsel, but also with strings of island flowers and shells.

"Starring" is a Christmas custom native to Alaska.

Merry Christmas to All

All too soon, our visit around the world must end. I hope you learned as much as I did and that you had fun along the way.

This Christmas, I'll be thinking of nisser, posadas and piñatas, and the picnicking in Australia. I'll be thinking also of how millions of people all over the world are decorating trees and setting up crèches—just like you and me!

Merry Christmas!

God Jul!
**Maria Jonsson
Sweden**

Joyeux Noël!
**Yan Sanchez
France**

축 성탄
**Chanmin Park and Youngeun Oh
Korea**

Merry Christmas!
Kat Stewart (and Miss Priss)
USA

¡Feliz Navidad!
Tony Castillo
El Salvador

Amezaliwa!
Marjory Mathangani
Kenya

Children's Workshop

Happy Holiday Crafts

Peppermint Ponies

Turn plain-Jane candy canes into holiday hobbyhorses. Hitch them to your tree or to presents for friends.

You will need (for each pony):
Pencil
Tracing paper
Scissors
2 (5″) squares of felt for the head
Scraps of felt for the eye and ear
5½″ piece of fringe
Tacky Glue
String
25½″ piece of ribbon
Paper clips (for holding glued pieces while they dry)
Star sequin
Candy cane

1. Trace and cut out the patterns.

2. Pin the head pattern to two layers of felt and cut out the heads. Cut a felt ear, eye, and pupil.

3. Cut away the loops on the fringe. Glue the fringe to the edge of one head. Cut a piece of string for a hanger and glue the ends to the top of the head.

4. Glue the edges of the second head to the first head, leaving the bottom edges open. Glue the ear and eye in place.

5. To make a halter, cut a 4½″ piece of ribbon. Wrap the ribbon around the horse's muzzle. Overlap the ends and glue them together. Cut the remaining ribbon in half. Glue one end of each ribbon to the underside of the muzzle ribbon. Glue a sequin to the halter. Let the glue dry.

6. Tie the loose ribbon ends into a bow. Gently slip the curved end of the candy cane into the cover, aiming the tip towards the horse's muzzle.

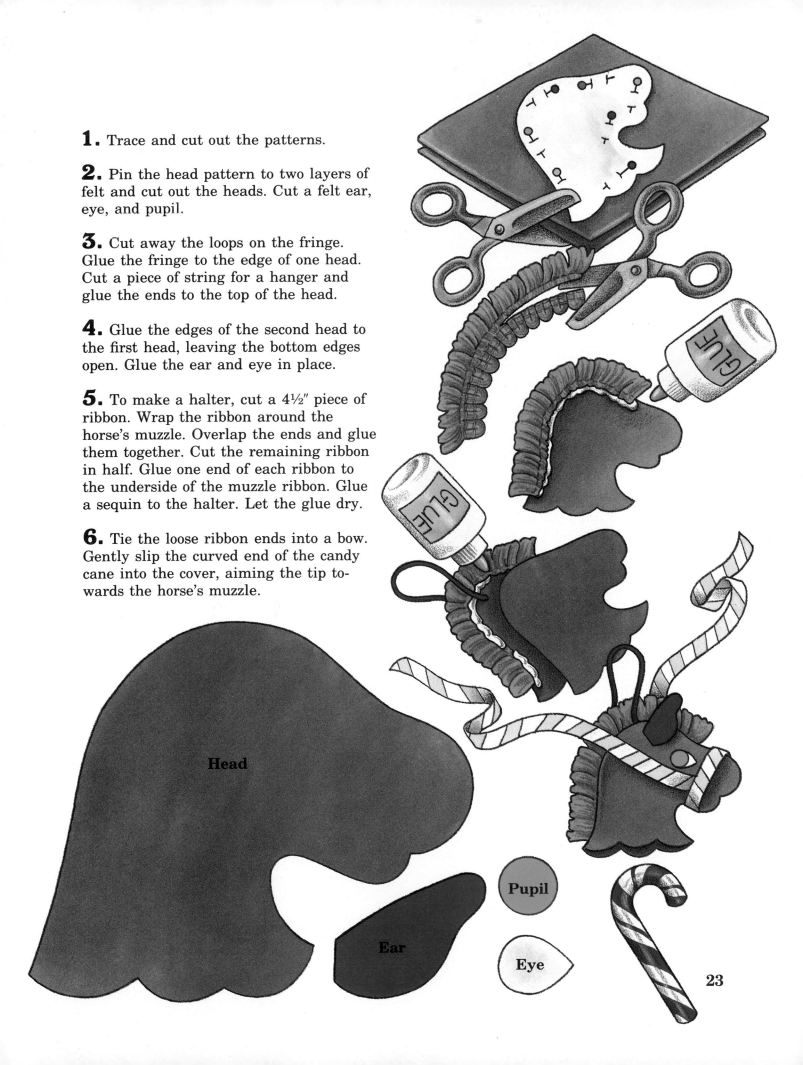

Head

Ear

Pupil

Eye

23

Cookie-Cutter Kids

Cinnamon and applesauce make these cookie look-a-likes smell as sweet as they look.

You will need:
3¾-ounce can of cinnamon plus extra for dusting
Applesauce
Large bowl
Tablespoon and mixing spoon
Waxed paper
Rolling pin and spatula
Small gingerbread-man cookie cutter
Toothpick and emery board
Slick pens
Buttons, beads, fabric scraps, rickrack, and other trim
White glue
Ribbon for hangers

1. Pour the can of cinnamon into the bowl. Add several tablespoons of applesauce and blend with the mixing spoon. Keep adding applesauce, a tablespoon at a time, to make a thick dough. Shape the dough into a ball.

2. Lightly dust a piece of waxed paper and the rolling pin with cinnamon. Place the ball of dough in the center of the paper. Flatten the ball with your hand and then roll it ¼" thick.

3. Using the cookie cutter, cut out the kids. Dust the spatula with cinnamon. Gently lift the kids and place them on a clean piece of waxed paper.

4. Use the toothpick to make a hole in the top of each kid. Let the kids dry for at least 24 hours, turning them often.

5. When the kids are thoroughly dry, sand any rough edges with the emery board. Decorate the kids and let dry.

6. Use ribbon for hangers.

Santa Cones

All of these are the same except for one thing. Which beard do you think suits Santa best?

You will need:
Pencil
Tracing paper
Scissors
Pink, black, and yellow construction paper
Red party hat (or paper cone)
White glue
Hole punch
Tiny red heart sticker
Cotton
White construction paper (optional)
White reinforcement tabs (optional)
Ornament hanger

1. Trace and cut out the patterns for the face and boot. Cut out one pink face and two black boots. Glue the face to the hat. Glue the tops of the boots to the inside of the hat.

2. Punch two black circles for eyes and glue them to the face. Stick a heart sticker below the eyes. For the beard, glue on cotton, curled paper strips, or paper curly-cues, or stick on reinforcement tabs. Trim the hat with cotton.

3. Cut a black strip for Santa's belt and a yellow rectangle for the buckle. Glue the buckle to the belt. Glue the belt in place. Let the glue dry.

4. Hang Santa on the tree with the ornament hanger.

26

Level 1

Face

Boot

27

Jumping Jack

Oh, how jolly this elf will be, dancing on your Christmas tree!

You will need:
Pencil
Tracing paper
Poster paper
Felt-tip markers
Scissors
Hole punch
8 small brads
Ribbon

1. Trace the patterns, pressing hard with your pencil.

2. Turn the tracings over and retrace them onto poster paper. Color the pieces.

3. Cut out the pieces. Punch a hole through each X. Assemble the pieces, using the brads.

4. Tie a ribbon around the jumping jack's cap and make a bow. Tie another ribbon to the cap ribbon for a hanger.

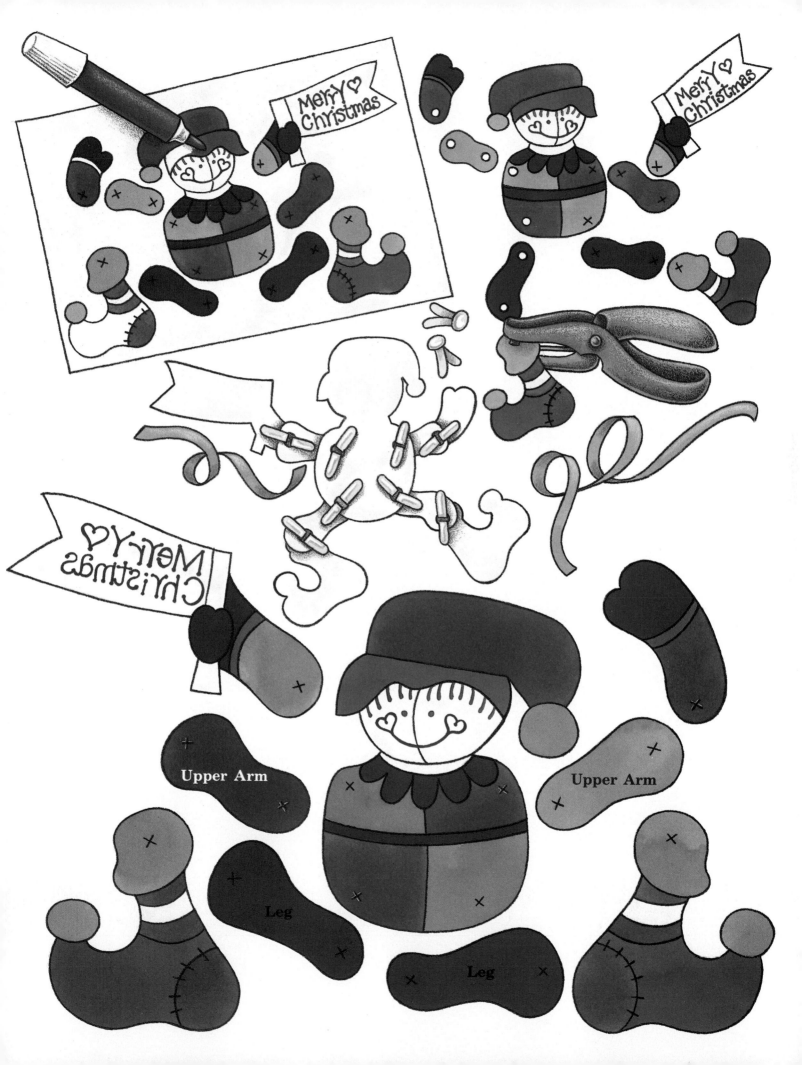

Upper Arm

Upper Arm

Leg

Leg

Cheery Trio

A rocking horse, a star, and a tree. Pick your favorite—or make all three!

You will need:
Pencil
Tracing paper
Scissors
White plastic-foam meat and vegetable trays
Acrylic paint and paintbrush
Felt cutouts, rickrack, yarn, stickers, and other trim
White glue
Ribbon

1. Trace and cut out the patterns. Draw around the patterns on the trays.

2. Cut out the ornaments, cutting along the outlines. Ask a grown-up to cut out the shapes inside the outlines with a craft knife.

3. Paint the ornaments, applying several coats of paint and letting the paint dry after each coat.

4. Trim the ornaments. Let dry.

5. Tie on pieces of ribbon for hangers.

Star

Horse

Tree

32

Paper Plate Angel

Snip, shape, and tape paper plates to make this angel. She'll look so pretty at the top of your tree!

Level 2

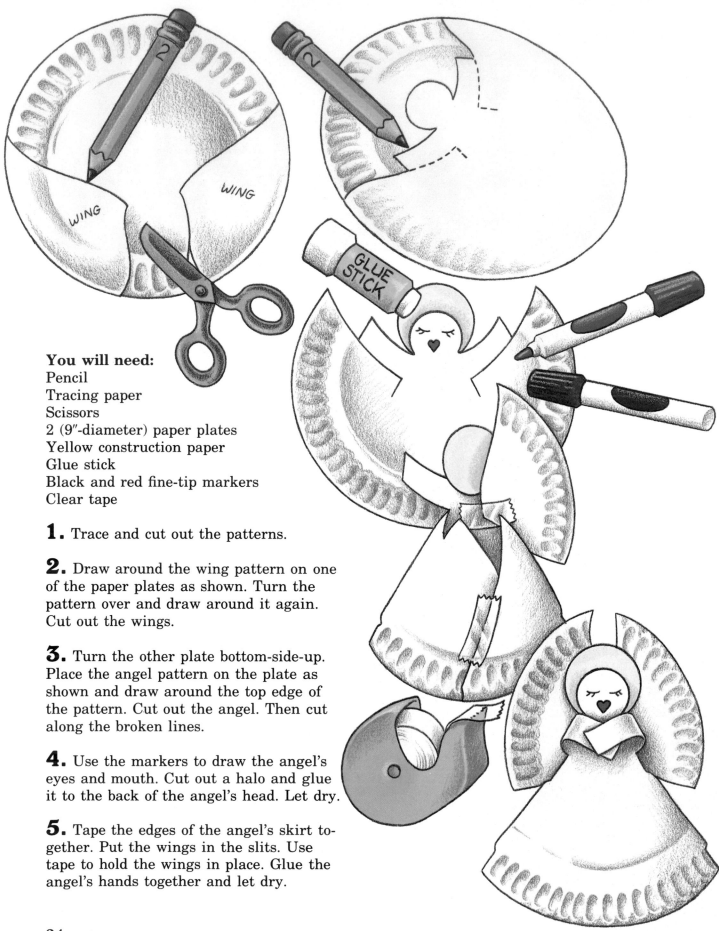

You will need:
Pencil
Tracing paper
Scissors
2 (9″-diameter) paper plates
Yellow construction paper
Glue stick
Black and red fine-tip markers
Clear tape

1. Trace and cut out the patterns.

2. Draw around the wing pattern on one of the paper plates as shown. Turn the pattern over and draw around it again. Cut out the wings.

3. Turn the other plate bottom-side-up. Place the angel pattern on the plate as shown and draw around the top edge of the pattern. Cut out the angel. Then cut along the broken lines.

4. Use the markers to draw the angel's eyes and mouth. Cut out a halo and glue it to the back of the angel's head. Let dry.

5. Tape the edges of the angel's skirt together. Put the wings in the slits. Use tape to hold the wings in place. Glue the angel's hands together and let dry.

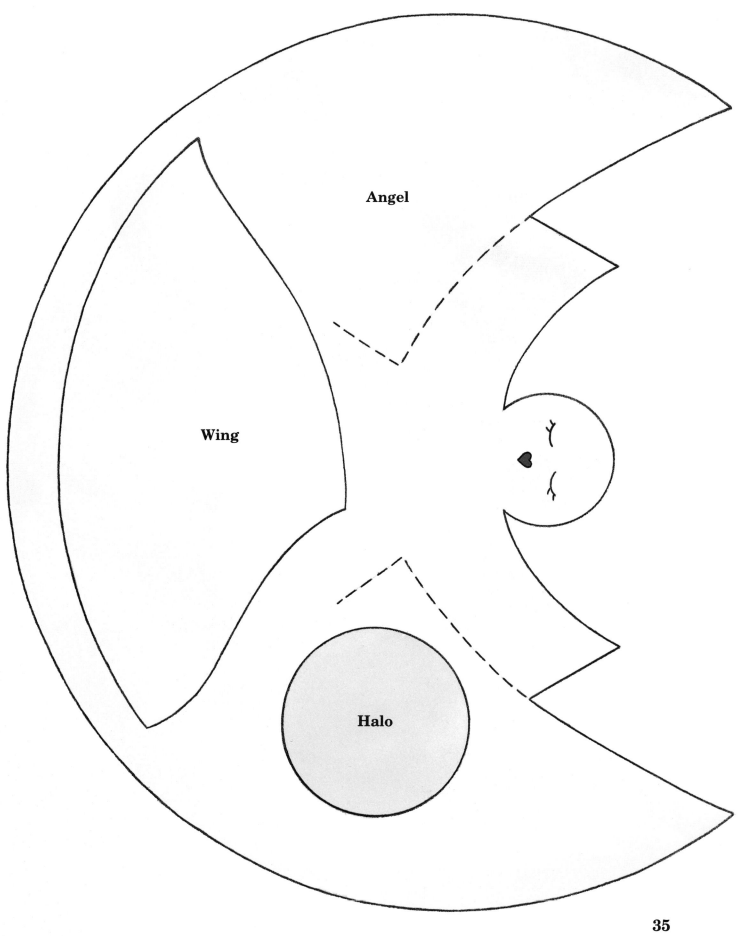

Angel

Wing

Halo

Shoe-Box Train

Load these cars with Christmas cards, candies, or pint-sized presents. Chug chug, toot toot—off they go!

You will need:
3 (child-size) shoe boxes and 2 lids
Wrapping paper
Scissors
Clear tape
2 small boxes (about 3″ x 3″ x 2″)
White glue
Pencil
Tracing paper
Paper towel roll
Poster paper
Paper for cutouts (optional)
Tape measure
1 yard of thick yarn
1″ wooden bead
Cotton balls

1. Wrap the shoe boxes with wrapping paper. Wrap the lids for the engine and caboose.

2. Wrap the small boxes and glue them to the engine and caboose lids.

3. Trace and cut out the pattern for the cowcatcher. Cut a smokestack and cowcatcher from the paper towel roll. Wrap these pieces and glue them to the engine.

4. Trace and cut out the patterns for the wheels and windows. Cut the wheels and windows from poster paper and glue them to the cars. Decorate the train with paper cutouts, if you like.

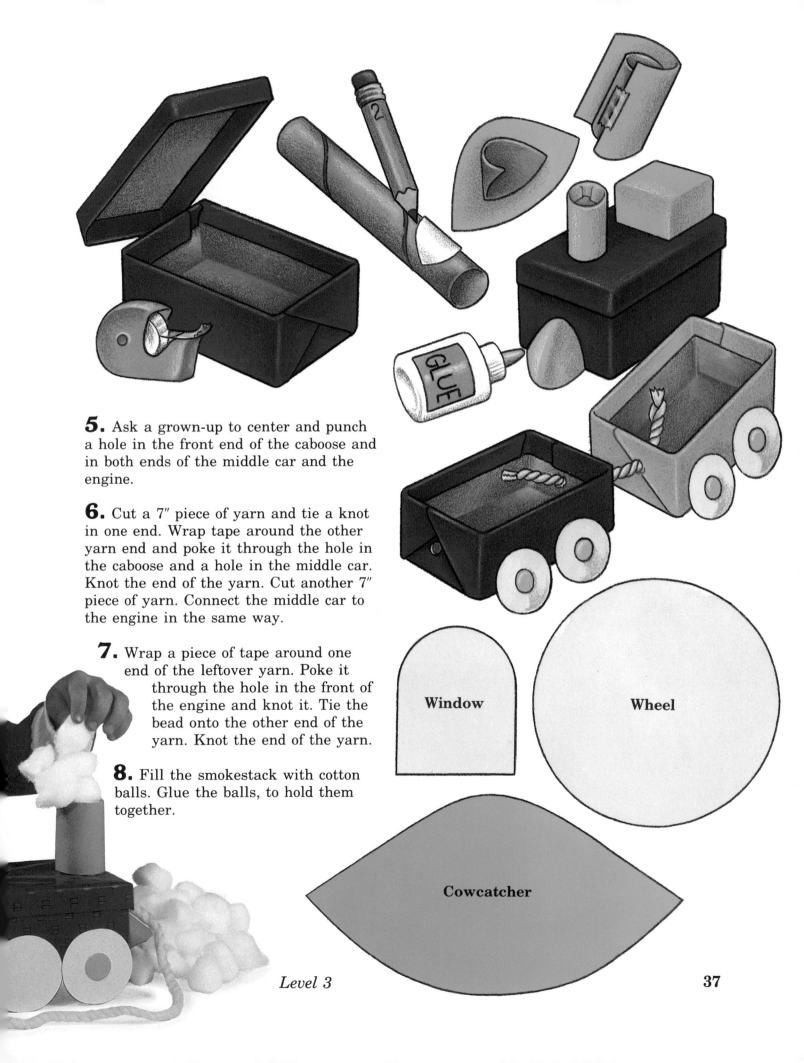

5. Ask a grown-up to center and punch a hole in the front end of the caboose and in both ends of the middle car and the engine.

6. Cut a 7″ piece of yarn and tie a knot in one end. Wrap tape around the other yarn end and poke it through the hole in the caboose and a hole in the middle car. Knot the end of the yarn. Cut another 7″ piece of yarn. Connect the middle car to the engine in the same way.

7. Wrap a piece of tape around one end of the leftover yarn. Poke it through the hole in the front of the engine and knot it. Tie the bead onto the other end of the yarn. Knot the end of the yarn.

8. Fill the smokestack with cotton balls. Glue the balls, to hold them together.

Window

Wheel

Cowcatcher

Window Wonderland

Use tissue paper cutouts to make a
stained-glass window. Watch it glow
when the sun shines through.

You will need:
Colored markers
Tissue paper
Scissors
Clear self-stick paper
Hole punch
Curling ribbon
Clear tape

1. Using the markers, draw holiday pictures on the tissue paper.

2. Cut out the pictures, leaving a border of tissue paper around each one.

3. Cut two pieces of self-stick paper big enough to cover each picture. Lay one piece of self-stick paper, sticky side up, on the table. Put the picture on top and cover it with the second piece of self-stick paper. Cut out the picture, following the outline.

4. Punch a hole in the top of each ornament. Pull a piece of ribbon through the hole and tie the ends to make a loop for hanging. Curl the ribbon ends.

5. Use tape to hang the ornaments in a window.

A Colorful Crèche

Silent night, holy night. Hang this special scene in your home to remind friends and family of the very first Christmas.

You will need:
Pencil
Tracing paper
White poster paper
Colored markers
Scissors
Glue stick
Slick pen (optional)
Tapestry needle
Narrow ribbon (about 1 yard)
Glitter

1. Trace all of the patterns, pressing hard with your pencil. To make the backs of the pieces, turn the tracings over and retrace them onto poster paper, pressing hard with your pencil. To make the fronts of the pieces, turn the tracing paper over again and retrace the patterns onto poster paper.

2. Color the pieces and cut them out.

3. Glue the pieces, except for the big stars, together. Trim the edges if necessary. Glue the big stars to the front and back of the cloud, lining up the edges.

4. Outline the pieces with the slick pen, if you like. Let dry.

Level 3

5. Use the needle to poke a hole through each X as marked on the patterns. Ask a grown-up to assemble the mobile, using ribbon to tie the pieces together.

6. Spread glue on the cloud, stars, angel wings, and Baby Jesus' halo. Sprinkle with glitter. When the glue is dry, shake off the glitter that did not stick.

Handy-Dandy Door Decoration

Here's a super idea for sprucing up your classroom door.

Level 1

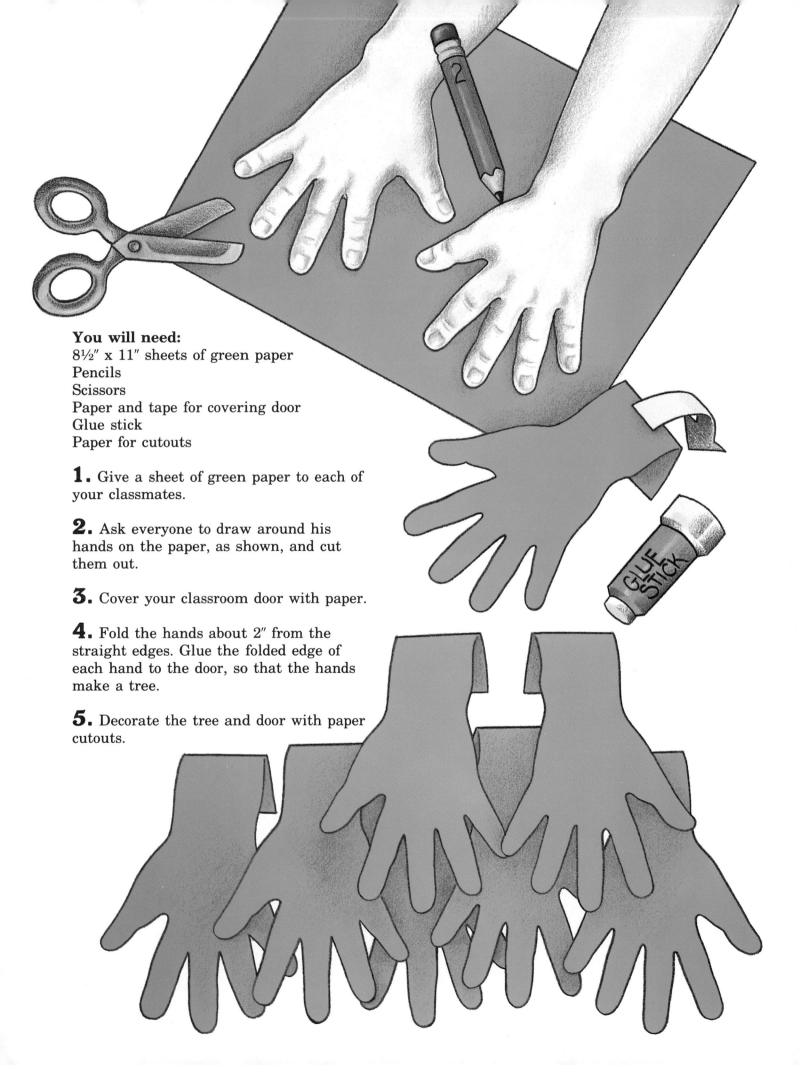

You will need:
8½″ x 11″ sheets of green paper
Pencils
Scissors
Paper and tape for covering door
Glue stick
Paper for cutouts

1. Give a sheet of green paper to each of your classmates.

2. Ask everyone to draw around his hands on the paper, as shown, and cut them out.

3. Cover your classroom door with paper.

4. Fold the hands about 2″ from the straight edges. Glue the folded edge of each hand to the door, so that the hands make a tree.

5. Decorate the tree and door with paper cutouts.

Sponge-Print Wrap

Sponge fun! Print your own paper. It's a wrapping that's almost too pretty to open.

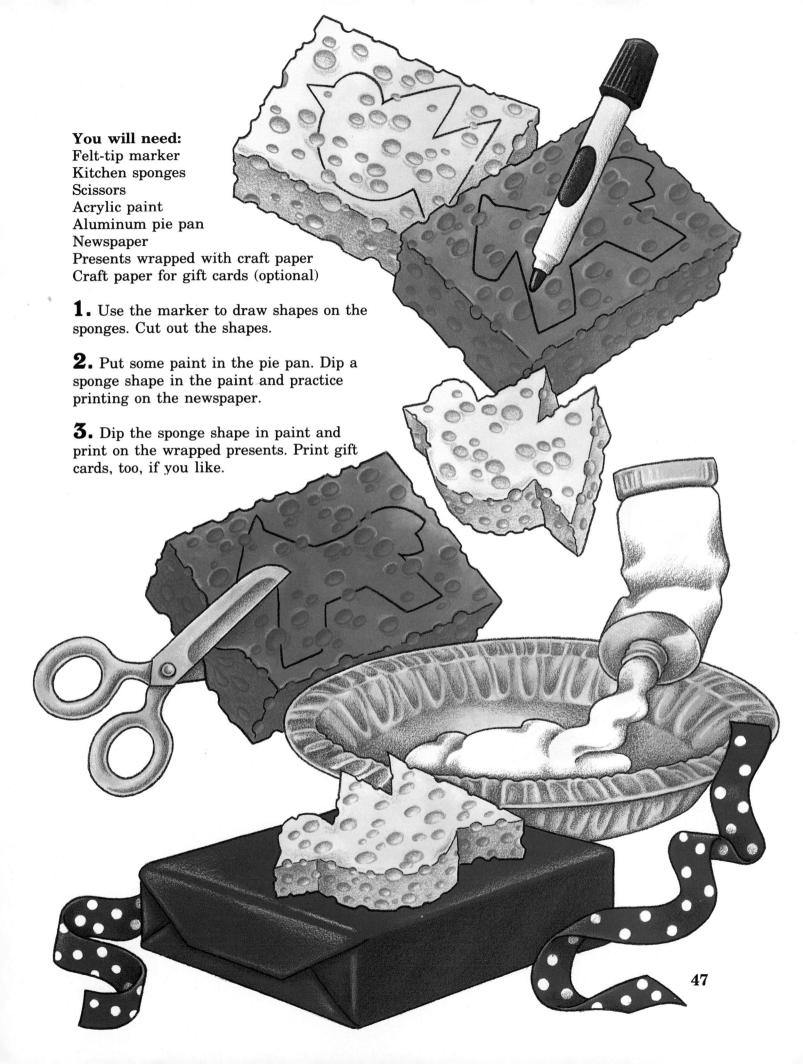

You will need:
Felt-tip marker
Kitchen sponges
Scissors
Acrylic paint
Aluminum pie pan
Newspaper
Presents wrapped with craft paper
Craft paper for gift cards (optional)

1. Use the marker to draw shapes on the sponges. Cut out the shapes.

2. Put some paint in the pie pan. Dip a sponge shape in the paint and practice printing on the newspaper.

3. Dip the sponge shape in paint and print on the wrapped presents. Print gift cards, too, if you like.

47

Reindeer Wrap

What a "deer" way to present a surprise!

You will need:
Pencil
Tracing paper
Scissors
Tan poster paper
Red and pink paper
Black felt-tip marker
Glue stick
Wrapped box
Clear tape

1. Trace and cut out the patterns for the reindeer you'd like to make.

2. On the tan poster paper, draw around the head, making the neck as long as you need it. (For the big reindeer, draw around the pattern, flip the pattern over, and draw around the pattern again to make one complete head.) Draw around the hoof twice.

3. Draw around the nose on red paper and draw around the cheek twice on pink paper. Cut out all of the pieces.

4. With the black marker, draw the eyes and mouth. Color the ears and hooves. Glue the cheeks and nose in place.

5. Glue the hooves to the front of the box. Glue the neck to the back of the box. Tape the neck to hold it securely. Let the glue dry.

Head

Nose

Cheek

Hoof

Head

Nose

Cheek

Hoof

Patchwork Cards

Once you catch on to making these cards, you can double the fun by designing your own.

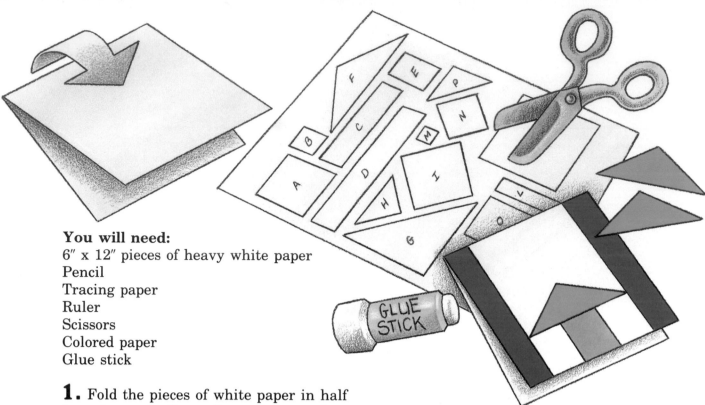

You will need:
6″ x 12″ pieces of heavy white paper
Pencil
Tracing paper
Ruler
Scissors
Colored paper
Glue stick

1. Fold the pieces of white paper in half to make cards. Trace the patterns, using the ruler to make your lines straight. Label and cut out the patterns.

Card 1
Use pattern A. Glue the red squares and then the green square.

Card 2
Use patterns B and C. Glue the squares and then the strips.

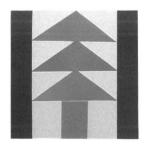

Card 3
Use patterns D, E, and F. Glue the red strips, the yellow strip, and then the triangles.

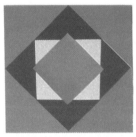

Card 4
Use patterns G, H, and I. Glue the yellow triangles, the purple triangles, and then the square.

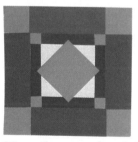

Card 5
Use patterns J, K, L, M, and N. Glue the medium-sized squares. Glue the purple strips, the small squares, the red strips, and then the big square.

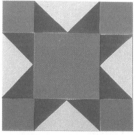

Card 6
Use patterns O, P, and Q. Glue the small squares. Glue the triangles and then the big square.

52

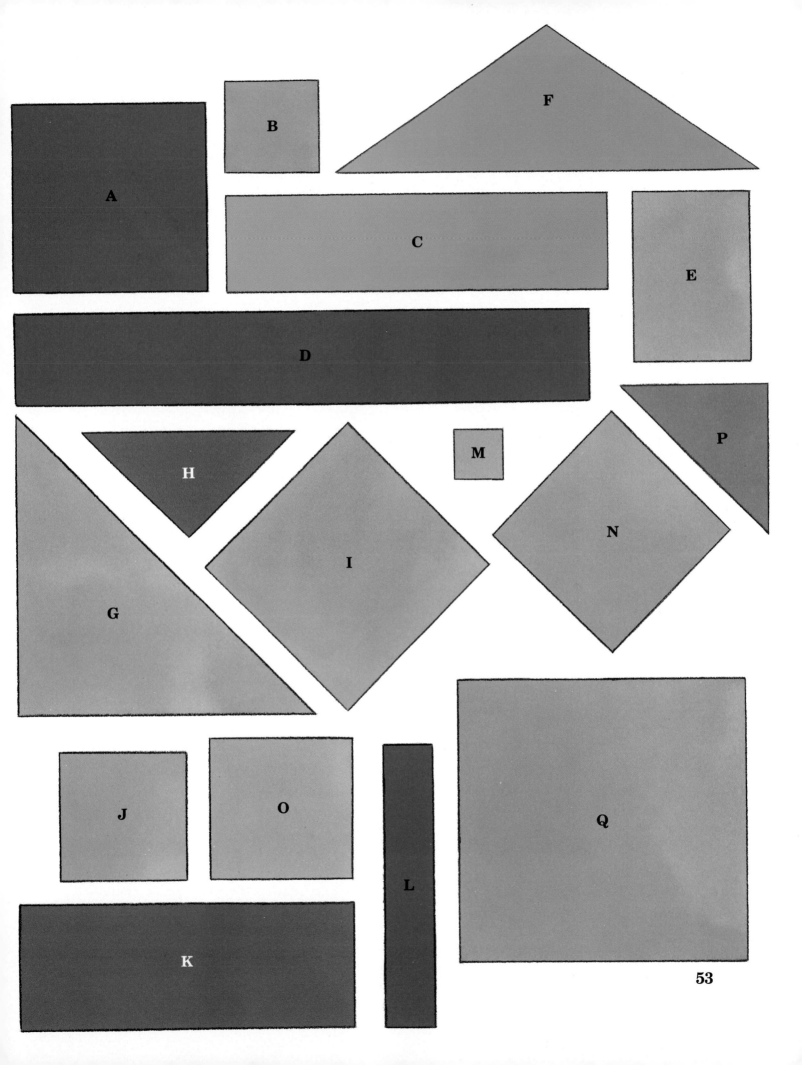

Cowboy Pete

Howdy, pardner! Packed with pencils, Pete will keep your buddies quick on the draw.

You will need:
Pencil
Tracing paper
Scissors
6″ x 12″ piece of poster paper
Felt
Tacky Glue
2 snaps for buttons
Star sticker
10″ piece of colored string

1. Trace and cut out all of the patterns.

2. Draw around the pattern for Pete on the poster paper. Draw around the other patterns on felt. Cut out the pieces.

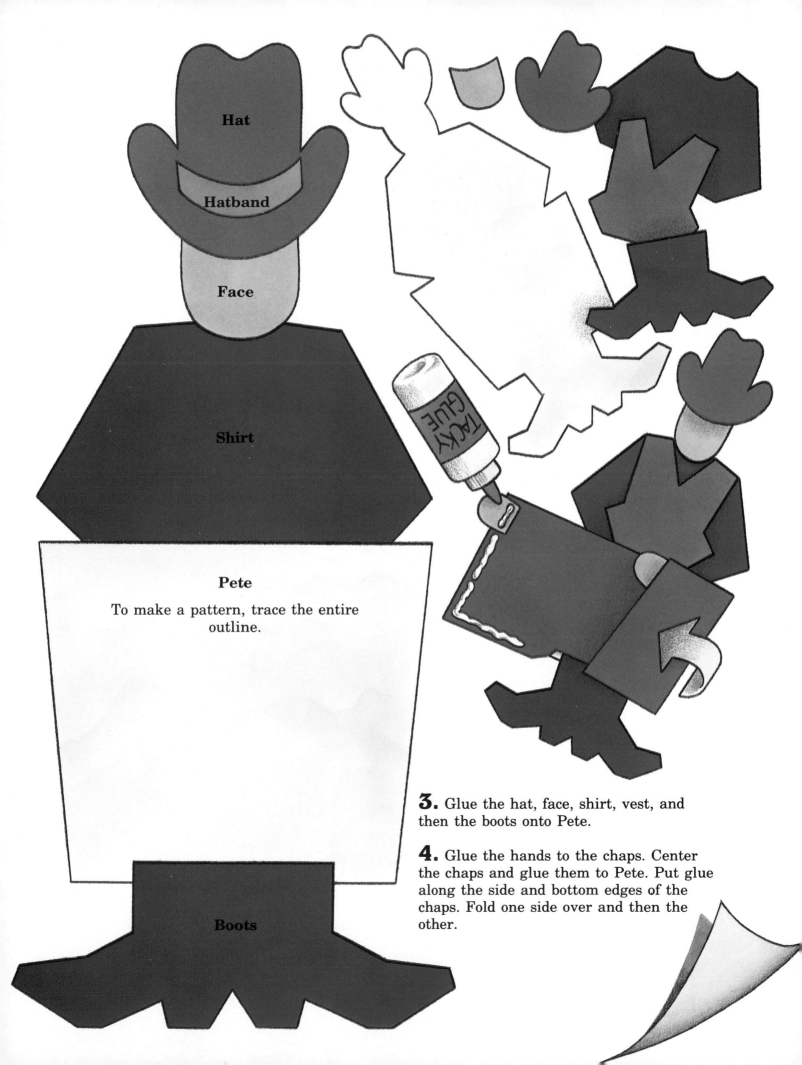

Hat

Hatband

Face

Shirt

Pete

To make a pattern, trace the entire outline.

Boots

TACKY GLUE

3. Glue the hat, face, shirt, vest, and then the boots onto Pete.

4. Glue the hands to the chaps. Center the chaps and glue them to Pete. Put glue along the side and bottom edges of the chaps. Fold one side over and then the other.

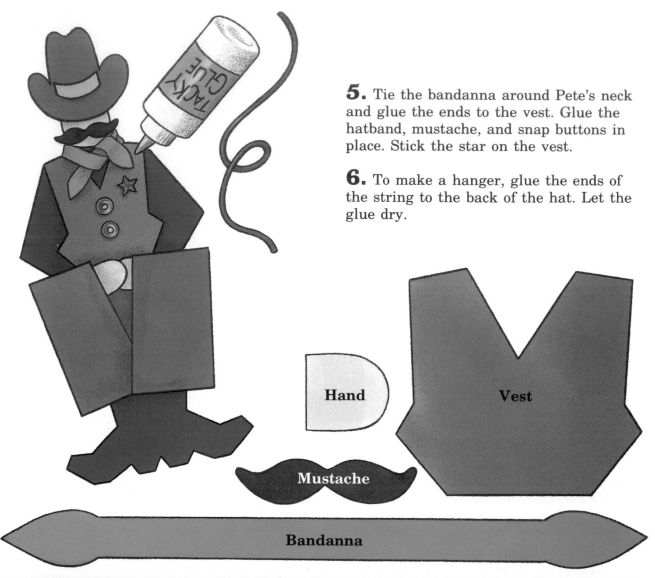

5. Tie the bandanna around Pete's neck and glue the ends to the vest. Glue the hatband, mustache, and snap buttons in place. Stick the star on the vest.

6. To make a hanger, glue the ends of the string to the back of the hat. Let the glue dry.

Hand

Vest

Mustache

Bandanna

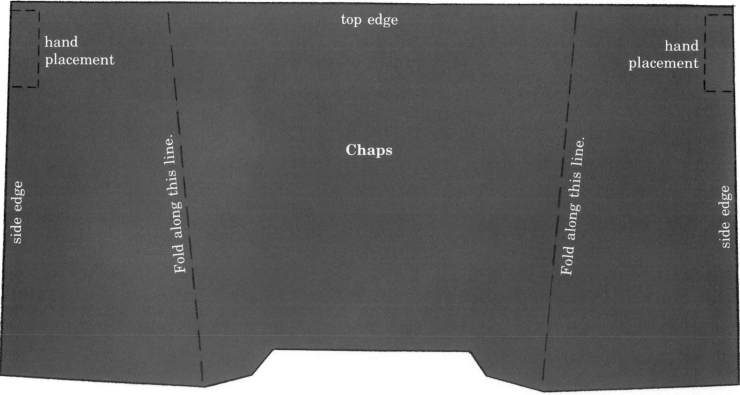

top edge

hand
placement

hand
placement

side edge

Fold along this line.

Chaps

Fold along this line.

side edge

Santa Claus Paperdolls

Did you ever wonder what Santa and Mrs. Claus wear in their spare time? Make plenty of these paperdoll sets. Pass them out for party favors or give them with colored markers for presents.

You will need:
Copy machine and paper (or lightweight card stock)
Gift sacks

1. Make copies of the dolls and clothes.

2. Divide the copies into sets and put a set in each sack.

Level 2

Stand
Cut 2 from poster paper. Glue the center section of one stand to the back of Santa's base. Glue the other stand to Mrs. Claus's base. Fold the ends toward the back.

Dolls
Before coloring, glue them to a piece of poster paper and let dry. Cut along the outlines.

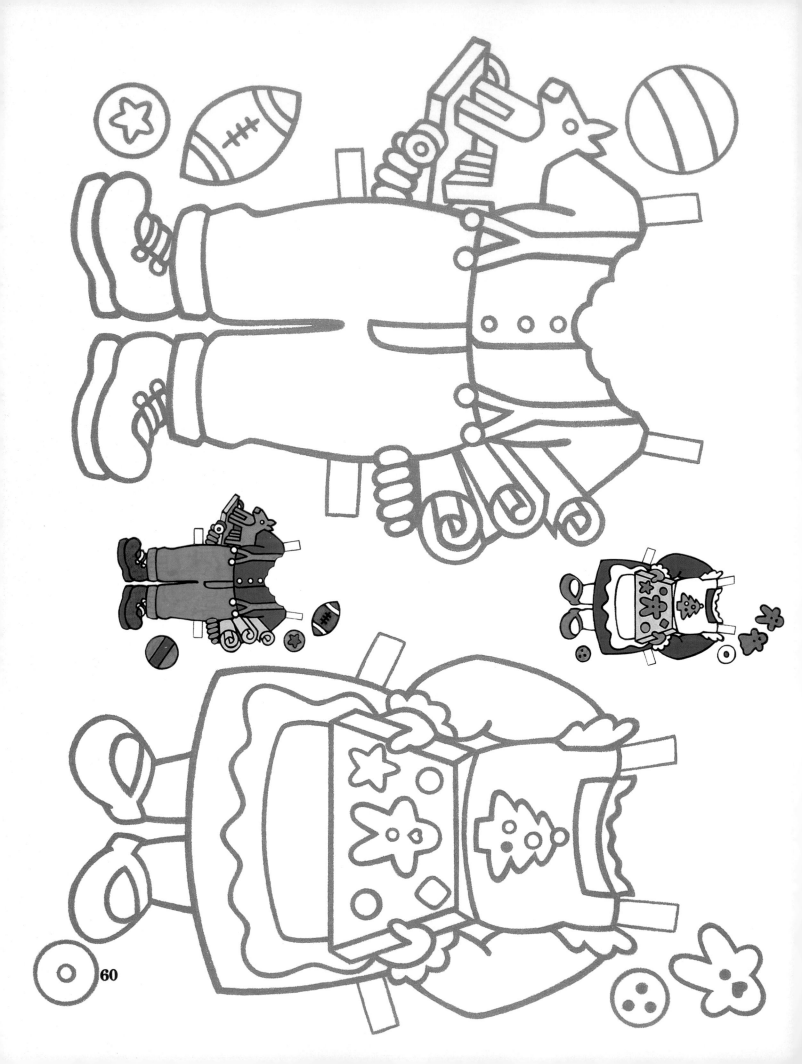

60

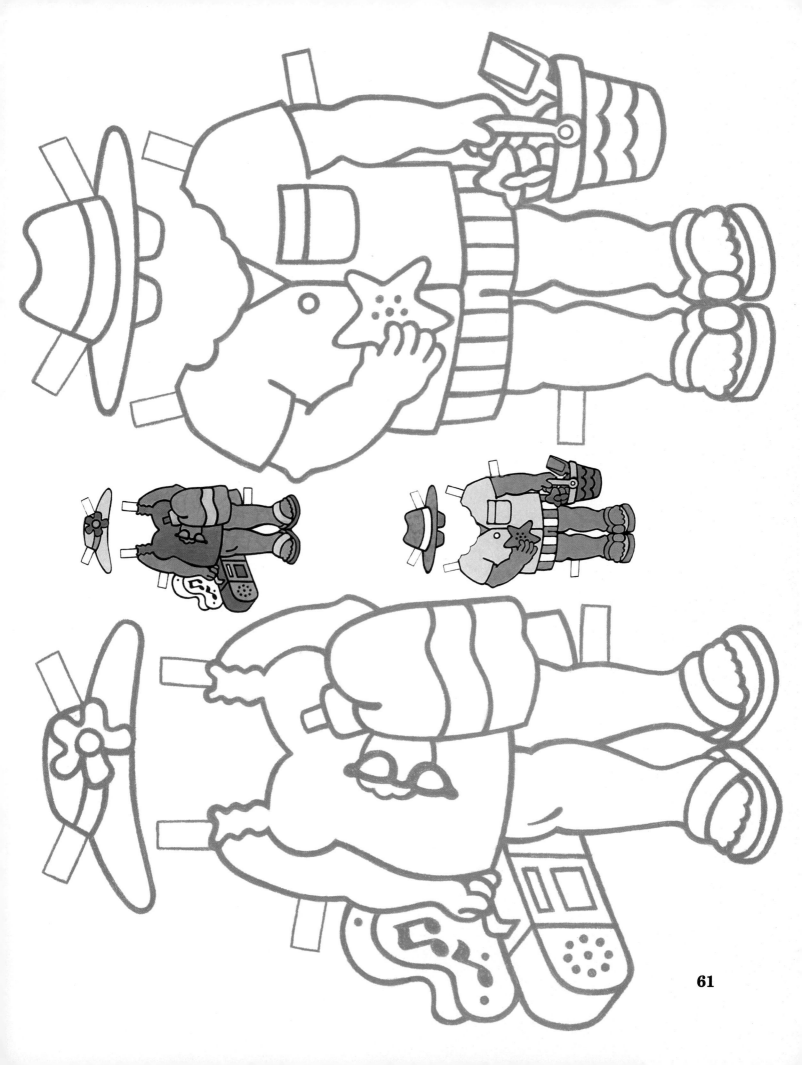

Nifty Necklaces

String straws and tiny packages to make a fashionable gift for your very best friend.

62

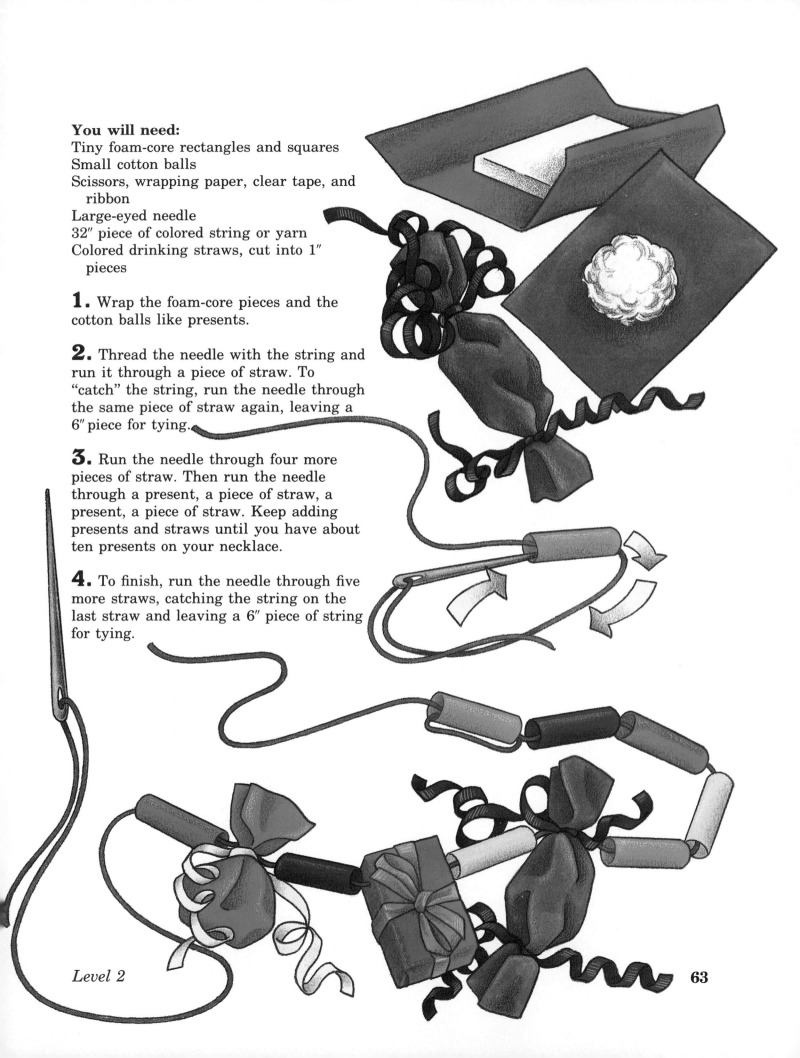

You will need:
Tiny foam-core rectangles and squares
Small cotton balls
Scissors, wrapping paper, clear tape, and
 ribbon
Large-eyed needle
32″ piece of colored string or yarn
Colored drinking straws, cut into 1″
 pieces

1. Wrap the foam-core pieces and the cotton balls like presents.

2. Thread the needle with the string and run it through a piece of straw. To "catch" the string, run the needle through the same piece of straw again, leaving a 6″ piece for tying.

3. Run the needle through four more pieces of straw. Then run the needle through a present, a piece of straw, a present, a piece of straw. Keep adding presents and straws until you have about ten presents on your necklace.

4. To finish, run the needle through five more straws, catching the string on the last straw and leaving a 6″ piece of string for tying.

Level 2

Hand-Painted Potholders

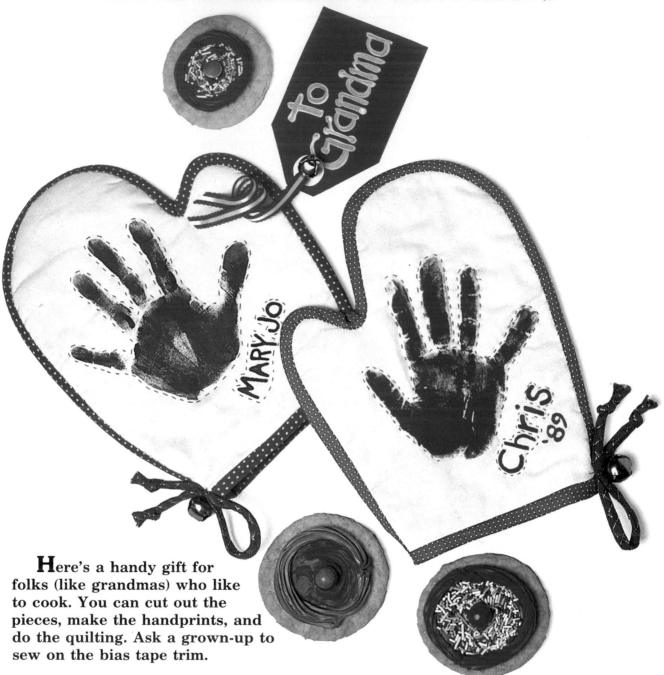

Here's a handy gift for folks (like grandmas) who like to cook. You can cut out the pieces, make the handprints, and do the quilting. Ask a grown-up to sew on the bias tape trim.

You will need (for each mitt):
Pencil
Tracing paper
Scissors
3 (9″ x 11″) pieces of bleached muslin
2 (9″ x 11″) pieces of polyester quilt batting

1 (9″ x 11″) piece of Christmas calico
Acrylic paint and wide paintbrush
Ballpoint paint tube
Large-eyed needle and quilting thread
1 yard extra-wide bias tape
12″ piece of decorative cording
¾″ jingle bell

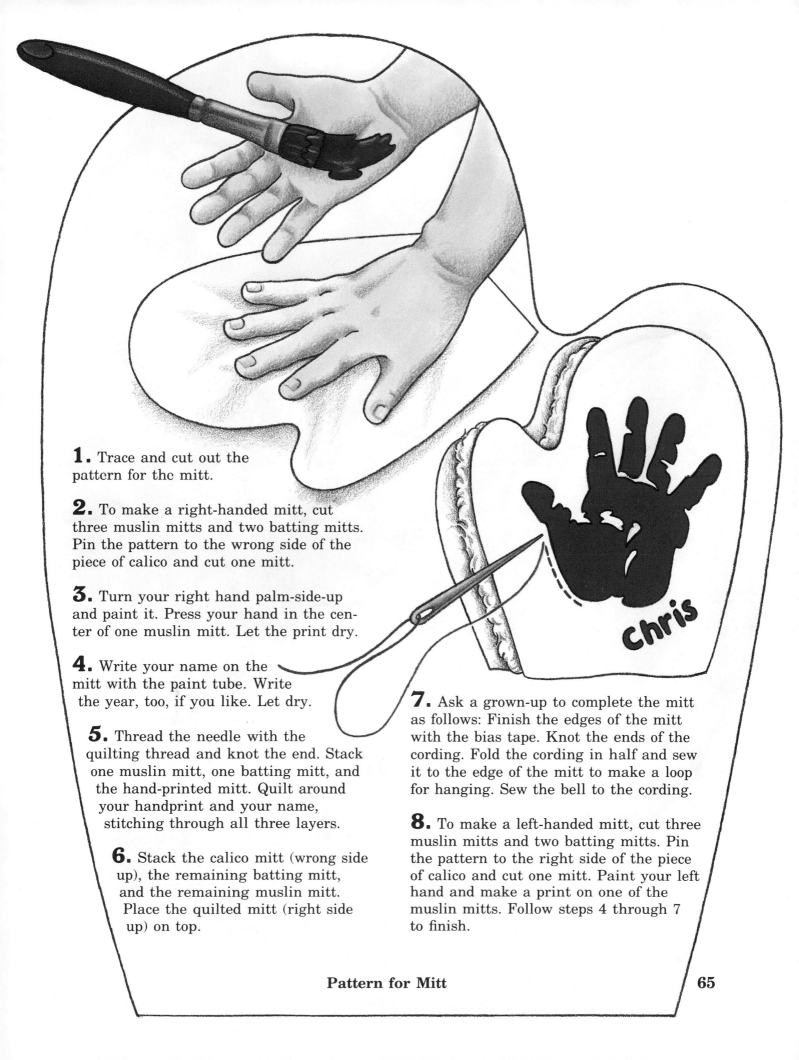

1. Trace and cut out the pattern for the mitt.

2. To make a right-handed mitt, cut three muslin mitts and two batting mitts. Pin the pattern to the wrong side of the piece of calico and cut one mitt.

3. Turn your right hand palm-side-up and paint it. Press your hand in the center of one muslin mitt. Let the print dry.

4. Write your name on the mitt with the paint tube. Write the year, too, if you like. Let dry.

5. Thread the needle with the quilting thread and knot the end. Stack one muslin mitt, one batting mitt, and the hand-printed mitt. Quilt around your handprint and your name, stitching through all three layers.

6. Stack the calico mitt (wrong side up), the remaining batting mitt, and the remaining muslin mitt. Place the quilted mitt (right side up) on top.

7. Ask a grown-up to complete the mitt as follows: Finish the edges of the mitt with the bias tape. Knot the ends of the cording. Fold the cording in half and sew it to the edge of the mitt to make a loop for hanging. Sew the bell to the cording.

8. To make a left-handed mitt, cut three muslin mitts and two batting mitts. Pin the pattern to the right side of the piece of calico and cut one mitt. Paint your left hand and make a print on one of the muslin mitts. Follow steps 4 through 7 to finish.

Pattern for Mitt

Stenciled Garden Gear

A hat and gloves will help a gardener keep cool and clean while working in the yard.

You will need:
Pencil
2½″ square of clear, heavyweight plastic
Clear tape
Straw hat
Red and green fine-point, waterproof
    markers
2 (#2) stencil brushes
Red and green stencil paint
Paper towels
Pair of gardening gloves
    1⅔ yards (1″-wide) green ribbon
        Glue stick
        1¼ yards (½″-wide) yellow ribbon
        1¼ yards (⅜″-wide) orange ribbon
            Small bouquet of red
                imitation flowers

Level 3

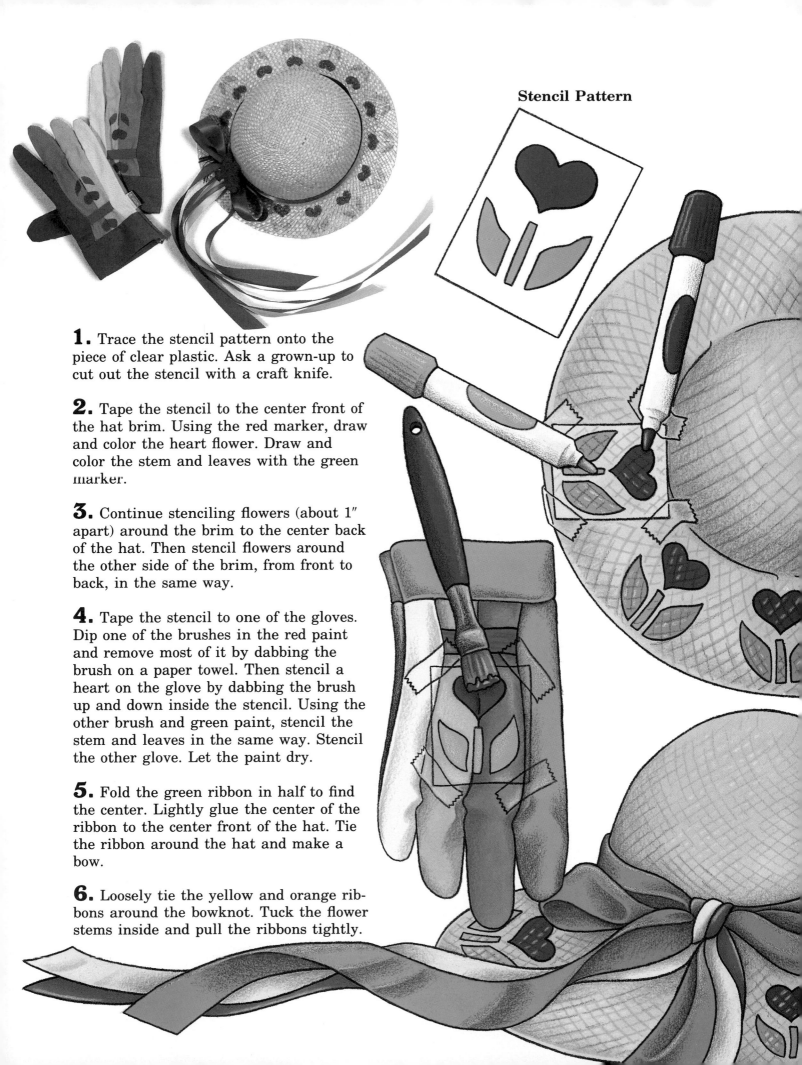

Stencil Pattern

1. Trace the stencil pattern onto the piece of clear plastic. Ask a grown-up to cut out the stencil with a craft knife.

2. Tape the stencil to the center front of the hat brim. Using the red marker, draw and color the heart flower. Draw and color the stem and leaves with the green marker.

3. Continue stenciling flowers (about 1″ apart) around the brim to the center back of the hat. Then stencil flowers around the other side of the brim, from front to back, in the same way.

4. Tape the stencil to one of the gloves. Dip one of the brushes in the red paint and remove most of it by dabbing the brush on a paper towel. Then stencil a heart on the glove by dabbing the brush up and down inside the stencil. Using the other brush and green paint, stencil the stem and leaves in the same way. Stencil the other glove. Let the paint dry.

5. Fold the green ribbon in half to find the center. Lightly glue the center of the ribbon to the center front of the hat. Tie the ribbon around the hat and make a bow.

6. Loosely tie the yellow and orange ribbons around the bowknot. Tuck the flower stems inside and pull the ribbons tightly.

Pet Stockings

Don't forget the family pets this Christmas. No bones about it—these stockings are purr-fect presents for them.

You will need (for each stocking):
Pencil
Tracing paper
Scissors
2 (8″ x 10½″) pieces of felt
Scraps of felt
Tacky Glue
Small button for eye
Sewing needle and thread
Tape measure
Ribbon
Jingle bell
Paper for tag (optional)
Pom-pom
3 star sequins

1. Trace and cut out the patterns for the stocking.

2. Pin the body pattern to the 8″ x 10½″ pieces of felt. Cut out the pieces.

3. From felt, cut a nose, heart cheek, and mouth. Cut the pocket and the pocket trim. Cut a tail if you're making the cat.

4. Glue the nose, heart cheek, and mouth in place. Sew on the button eye.

5. Glue the pocket trim to the pocket. Put glue on the side and bottom edges of the pocket and position it on the stocking. Glue the cat's tail in place. Let the glue dry.

6. Thread the needle and tie the ends of the thread together. Using a running stitch, sew the body pieces together, following the broken lines on the pattern.

7. Cut a 28″ piece of ribbon and thread the bell midway between the ends. Make a name tag if you like. Tie the ribbon around the pet stocking's neck.

8. Glue the pom-pom and star sequins in place. Let the glue dry.

9. To make a loop for hanging, tie a piece of ribbon to the neck ribbon.

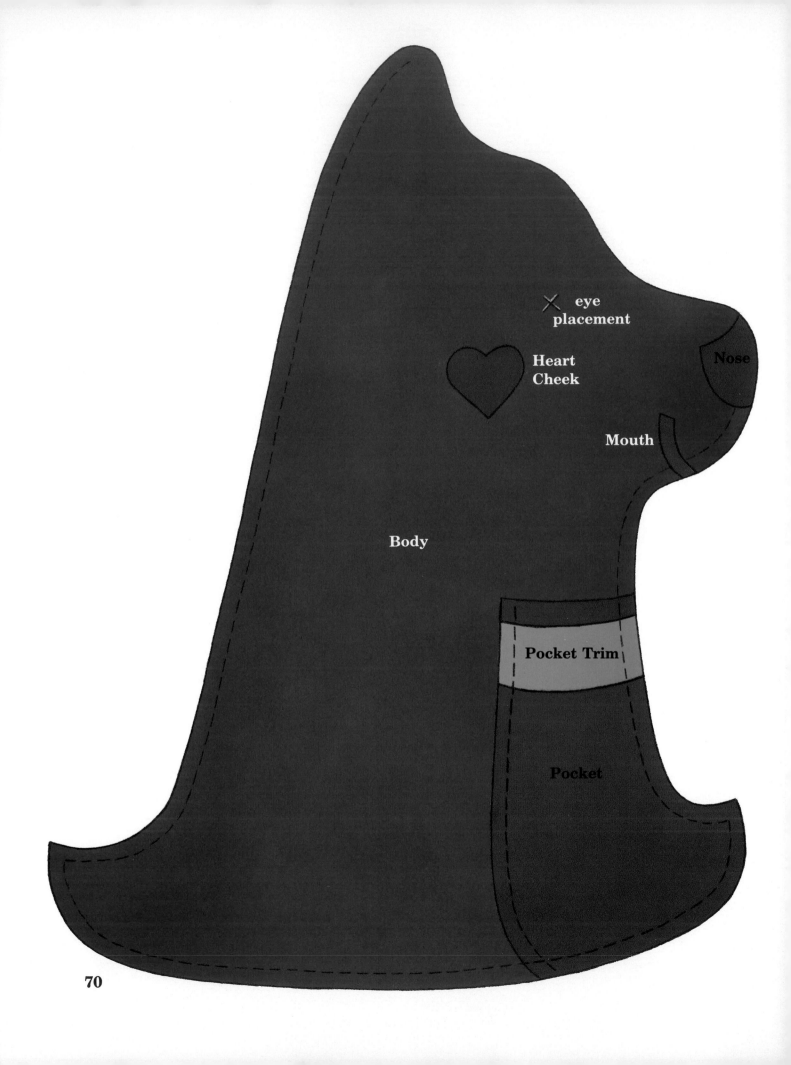

eye
placement

Heart
Cheek

Nose

Mouth

Body

Pocket Trim

Pocket

70

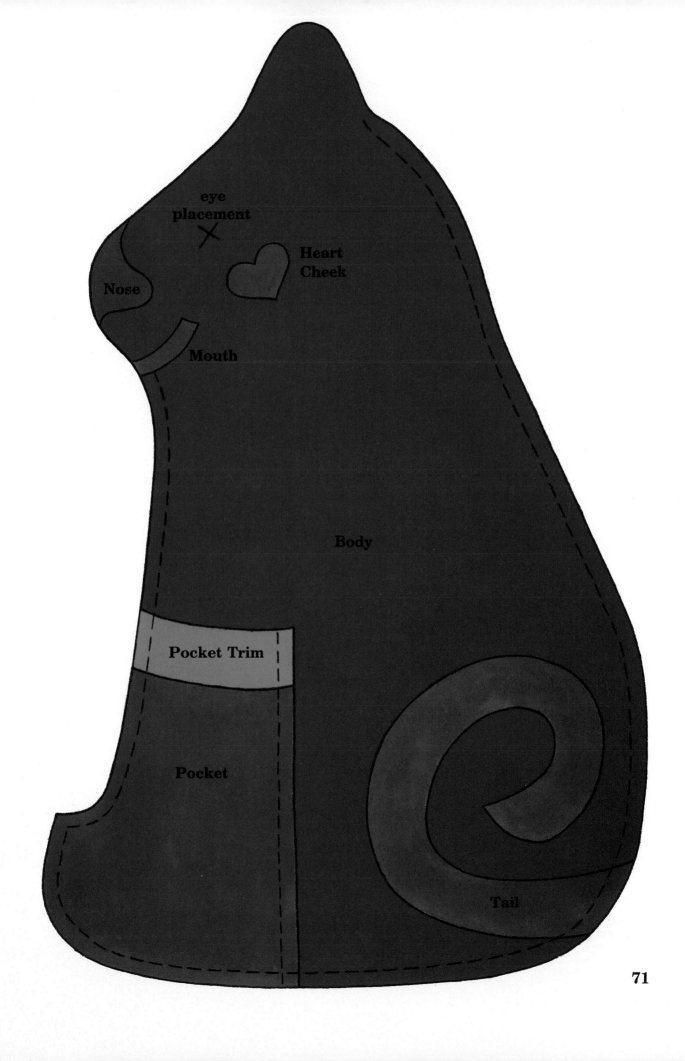

eye placement

×

Nose

Heart Cheek

Mouth

Body

Pocket Trim

Pocket

Tail

Parents' Workshop
Great Gifts for Children

Chris-Mouse Sleep Set

For perfect pictures on Christmas morning, give her a new nightie on Christmas Eve. Holiday hearts and bows and a tiny Christmas mouse dress up this version, which will appear even merrier with slippers to match.

Note: Use matching thread and narrow satin stitch to appliqué pieces. Use scant ⅛" seam allowance when sewing mice for slippers.

Nightshirt
You will need:
5" x 5" piece of gray velour knit fabric
10" x 12" piece of red pindot fabric
5" x 7" piece of red-and-white striped fabric
Thread to match
¼ yard of lightweight fusible interfacing
Nightshirt
Embroidery needle
Red and black embroidery floss
4" (¼"-wide) gray grosgrain ribbon (tail)
2 yards (¾"-wide) Christmas ribbon
1 red bow button
1 red heart button
1 small jingle bell

1. Cut outer ears from velour knit as marked. Fuse pieces of interfacing to wrong side of the remaining fabric pieces. Cut inner ears and hearts from pindot, candy canes from striped fabric, and remaining mouse pieces from velour knit, as marked.

2. Appliqué inner ears to right side of a pair of outer ears. With right sides together, sew appliquéd ears to plain ears, using ⅛" seam allowance and leaving bottom edges open. Turn ears right side out and baste to wrong side of face.

3. Referring to photo, determine placement of appliqués on nightshirt. (Note: Pindot and candy cane hearts are appliquéd on back of nightshirt, at bottom, same as front.) Cut a piece of interfacing large enough to back each appliqué and fuse to wrong side of nightshirt.

4. Appliqué mouse body, tucking one end of ribbon tail under edge. Appliqué remaining pieces as follows: paw on left, small candy cane, paw on right, face, and then hearts on shirt bottom.

5. Embroider mouse's face as marked on pattern, using two strands of floss. Sew bow button to ear. Tie a knot at end of ribbon tail. Fold tail about 1½" from end and tack to nightshirt.

6. Cut two 10" pieces of Christmas ribbon and cut Vs in ends. Tie the ribbons into bows; tack to sleeves at cuffs. Make a six-loop bow with the remaining ribbon; cut Vs in the ends. Sew heart button and bell to center of bow. Tack bow to nightshirt at neck.

Slippers
You will need:
7" x 10" piece of gray velour knit fabric
Scrap of red pindot fabric
Thread to match
Polyester stuffing
Sewing needle
4 black beads for eyes
Hot-glue gun and glue stick
Fabric glue
2 tiny red pom-poms
2 tiny green bows
½ yard (¾"-wide) Christmas ribbon
2 small jingle bells
Slippers

1. Transfer patterns to fabrics and cut as marked.

2. To make each mouse, appliqué inner ears to pair of outer ears, using satin stitch and matching thread. With right sides together, sew appliquéd ears to pair of plain ears, leaving openings as marked. Turn ears right side out.

3. Sew face pieces, right sides together, at center front. Lightly pleat ears. With appliquéd side down and round edges toward center of face, baste ears to right side of face as marked. With right sides together, sew face to back of head, leaving opening as marked. Turn mouse right side out and stuff; sew opening closed.

4. Using sewing needle and double thread, sew on bead eyes, sewing from bead to bead through head and pulling thread slightly to indent face.

5. Glue heart cheeks with fabric glue. Use hot glue to attach pom-pom nose and tiny bow (to ear). Cut Christmas ribbon in half. Tie a bow with each piece and sew bell to center. Hot-glue a mouse and bow to each slipper. Let the glue dry.

Patterns for Slippers

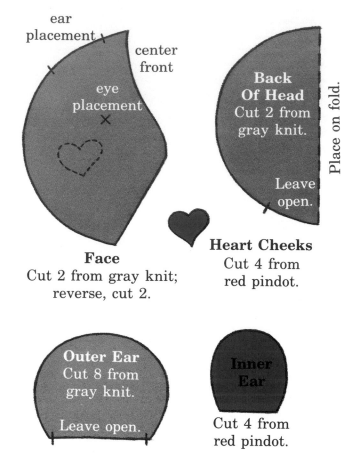

ear placement

center front

eye placement

Face
Cut 2 from gray knit;
reverse, cut 2.

Back Of Head
Cut 2 from gray knit.

Leave open.

Place on fold.

Heart Cheeks
Cut 4 from red pindot.

Outer Ear
Cut 8 from gray knit.

Leave open.

Inner Ear
Cut 4 from red pindot.

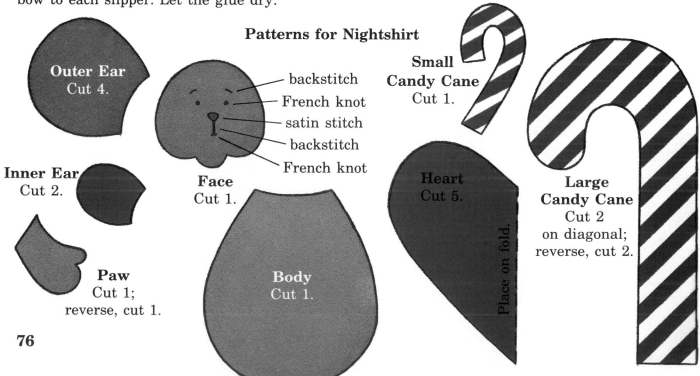

Patterns for Nightshirt

Outer Ear
Cut 4.

Inner Ear
Cut 2.

Paw
Cut 1;
reverse, cut 1.

Face
Cut 1.

backstitch
French knot
satin stitch
backstitch
French knot

Body
Cut 1.

Heart
Cut 5.

Small Candy Cane
Cut 1.

Large Candy Cane
Cut 2 on diagonal;
reverse, cut 2.

Place on fold.

76

Cow Sweater

Outstanding in black and white, Bossy lends this sweater a boldness that's bound to appeal to country kids and city slickers, too. A project for intermediate knitters, this one should be a pleasure for those familiar with graphs and the ins and outs of changing yarns.

You will need:

Sizes 4 and 8 knitting needles
Size 4 circular knitting needle
Bobbins (optional)
Stitch holder
Tapestry needle
Sportweight yarn: 5 (6, 8) 50-gram skeins royal blue for size small (medium, large); 1 (50-gram) skein each white and black; small amount of pink for ears, nostrils, and udder; small amount of green for grass
11″ (⅜″-wide) red grosgrain ribbon
Small cowbell
Black thread

Standard Knitting Abbreviations

st(s)—stitch(es)
St st—stockinette stitch
K—knit
P—purl
beg—begin(ning)
dec—decrease(s)
inc—increase(s)
rem—remain(ing)

Sizing Chart

	S	M	L
Chest (actual)	25"	27"	29"
Chest (finished)	30"	32"	34"
Length (shoulder to hip)	17½"	19½"	21½"
Sleeve length	12"	15"	16"

Gauge: 4 sts and 6 rows = 1" in St st on larger needles. Work a sample on suggested-size needles to check your tension before beginning the project. If swatch is too tight, change to larger needles; if too loose, change to smaller needles. Gauge must be accurate for proper fit.

Note: Since it is best not to carry thread over more than two stitches, it may be easier to wind yarn on bobbins while working the graph. To avoid holes, twist old yarn over new when changing colors. Directions are given for size small. Directions for sizes medium and large are in parentheses.

Back: With smaller needles and royal blue, cast on 60 (64, 68) sts. Work in K 1, P 1 ribbing for 2½". Change to larger needles and work in St st until piece measures 17½" (19½", 21½") from beg. Bind off loosely.

Front: Work ribbing as for back. Change to larger needles and work in St st according to graph. Follow graph for proper size and color changes. When piece measures 14½" (16½", 18½") from beg, shape neckline (graph should be completed).

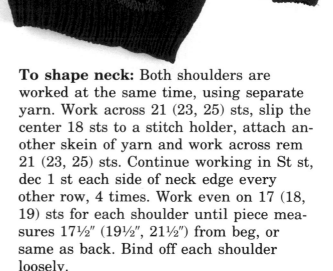

To shape neck: Both shoulders are worked at the same time, using separate yarn. Work across 21 (23, 25) sts, slip the center 18 sts to a stitch holder, attach another skein of yarn and work across rem 21 (23, 25) sts. Continue working in St st, dec 1 st each side of neck edge every other row, 4 times. Work even on 17 (18, 19) sts for each shoulder until piece measures 17½" (19½", 21½") from beg, or same as back. Bind off each shoulder loosely.

Sleeves: With smaller needles and royal blue, cast on 32 sts (same for medium and large). Work in K 1, P 1 ribbing for 2". Change to larger needles and work in St st. Inc 1 st each end of needle, every 5th row, 15 times, until 62 (66, 70) sts are on needle. Work even until sleeve measures 12½" (15", 16½") from beg. Bind off loosely. Rep for second sleeve.

To finish: Using tapestry needle and matching yarn, weave shoulder seams. For neck, with royal blue and circular needle, pick up 60 (60, 72) sts. Work in K 1, P 1 ribbing for 1". Bind off loosely in rib pattern.

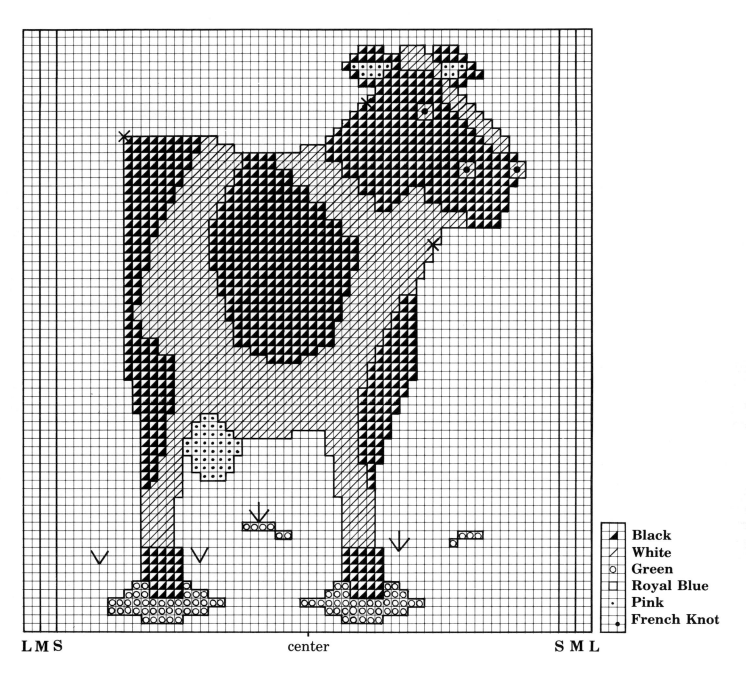

Black
White
Green
Royal Blue
Pink
French Knot

To attach sleeves, match center top of sleeve to shoulder seam. Weave sleeve to sweater body. Weave sleeve seam from wrist to underarm. Weave sweater side seam from waist to underarm.

Referring to graph, use tapestry needle and pink yarn to make a French knot in each nostril. Use black yarn to make a French knot for the eye. With green, embroider extra blades of grass.

Thread bell to midpoint of ribbon and secure with a knot. Thread ends of ribbon through sweater at points on neck indicated on graph; tack ends together.

For tail, cut six 10″ lengths of black yarn. Tie them together at one end and braid for 5½″ or desired length. Wrap end of braid with black thread, knotting to secure. Fray end of tail and trim if desired. Thread top of tail through sweater at point indicated on graph. Tack to sweater on inside.

Blue-Ribbon Bibs

Set the stage for mealtime fun
with a trio of cute and colorful bibs.
Made from the same basic pattern,
these easy-care bibs are quick to sew.
And if you're a scrap saver, check
your stash. No doubt, you've usable
fabrics already at hand.

Note: Pattern for bib includes ¼" seam
allowances. Refer to the photographs for
placement of trim and appliqués.

Clown Bib
You will need:
⅓ yard (45″-wide)
  polka-dot poly/
  cotton
⅓ yard (45″-wide) white
  poly/cotton (for lining)
⅓ yard (½″-wide) red bias tape
Thread to match
1 yard (¼″-wide) red grosgrain ribbon
2 (1½″-diameter) red pom-poms

1. Cut bib pieces as marked.

2. To make ruffle, cut a 4″ x 12″ strip from remaining white fabric. Pin and stitch bias tape to one long edge. Press ends of strip under ¼″ and then ¼″ again; stitch, sewing close to edges. Run a line of gathering stitches ¼″ from raw edge; gather to fit bib neck.

3. Lay bib front right side up. Pin wrong side of ruffle to neck, aligning raw edges. Cut ribbon in half and pin one end of each piece to neck, 1″ in from either side. (See figure.) Lay bib lining, right side down, on top; stitch all around, leaving 3″ opening for turning. Turn bib right side out and press; sew opening closed.

4. Sew pom-poms securely to bib front.

Indian Bib
You will need:
⅔ yard (45″-wide) flesh-colored poly/cotton
  (for bib front and lining)
⅓ yard tan poly/cotton
Scraps of red and yellow cotton fabrics
22″ (½″-wide) green bias tape
½ yard (½″-wide) blue bias tape
½ yard (1″-wide) red fringe trim
½ yard (½″-wide) yellow rickrack
1 yard (¼″-wide) red grosgrain ribbon
Thread to match

1. Cut bib and vest pieces as marked. Sew vest pieces to bib front, aligning side edges. Cut moons and arrows from scraps.

2. Cut green bias tape in half and stitch to front of vest, sewing down long edges of each piece. Position and appliqué the moons and arrows. Cut five 2″ pieces of blue bias tape and arrange in zigzag fashion on one side of vest, trimming pieces to fit if necessary; pin and stitch. Repeat for other side of vest. Pin fringe along bottom edge of bib front, aligning straight edge with bib edge.

3. Follow step 3 under Clown Bib, omitting the ruffle.

4. Topstitch rickrack to bottom edge of the vest.

Sheriff Bib
You will need:
⅓ yard (45″-wide) blue denim
⅓ yard (45″-wide) red polka-dot
  fabric (for lining)
Piece of red bandanna
Scraps of yellow and light gray cotton
  fabrics
Red, yellow, and dark gray thread
1 yard (¼″-wide) red grosgrain ribbon
3 brass buttons

1. Cut bib pieces as marked. Cut denim pocket and appliqué pieces.

2. Beginning at center bottom edge of bib front, lightly draw a 7″ line up center. Set machine for satin stitch. Using red thread, stitch along line. Position and pin bandanna, star, and gun. Appliqué pieces, using matching thread.

3. Press under all pocket edges ¼″. Using red thread, machine-stitch across top of pocket, ¼″ from edge. Stitch pocket to bib, sewing ¼″ in from side and bottom edges.

4. Follow step 3 under Clown Bib, omitting the ruffle.

5. Sew buttons securely to bib, to right of center stitching.

Bandanna

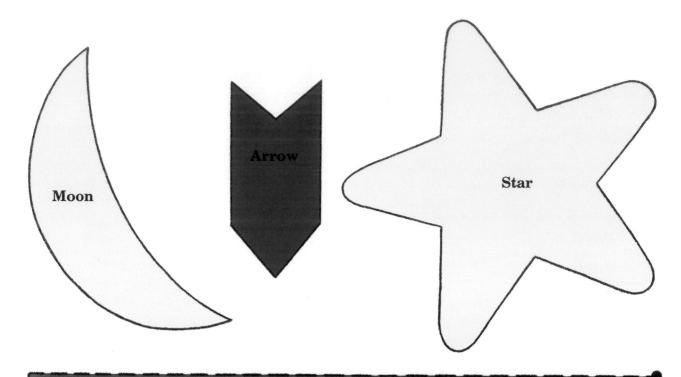

Moon

Arrow

Star

Place on fold.

Cut here for Indian vest pieces.

Bib
For clown, cut 1 polka-dot and 1 white on
fold.
For sheriff, cut 1 denim and 1 polka-dot
on fold.
For Indian, cut 2 flesh-colored on fold and
2 tan vest pieces.
(Pattern includes ¼″ seam allowance.)

**Match dots and continue pattern
across page.**

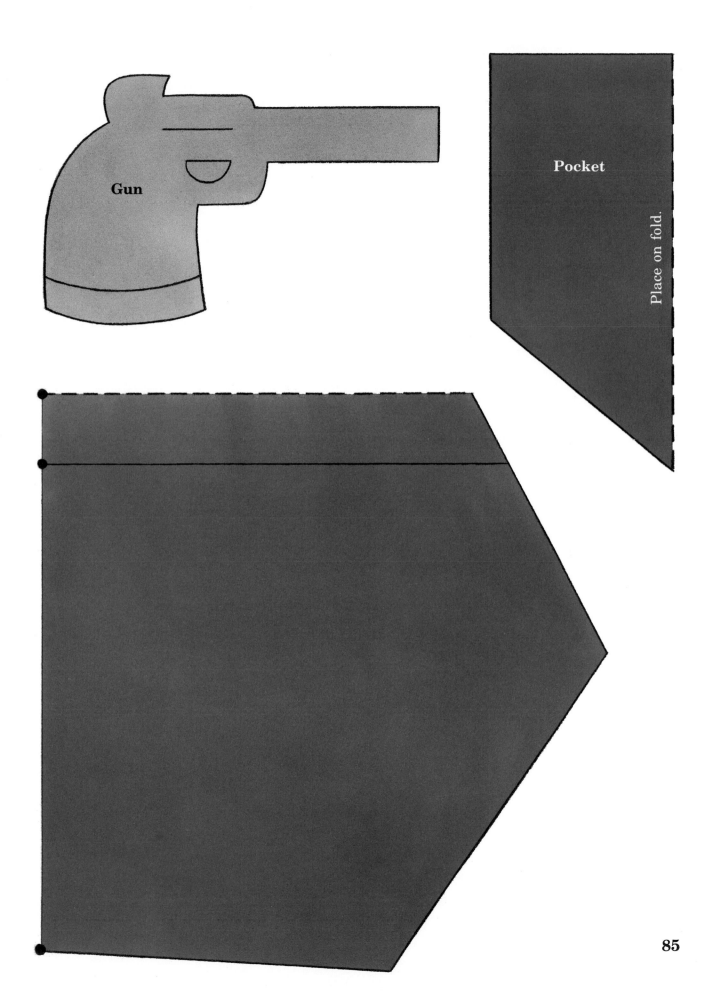

Gun

Pocket

Place on fold.

Pocket Pony Sweatsuit

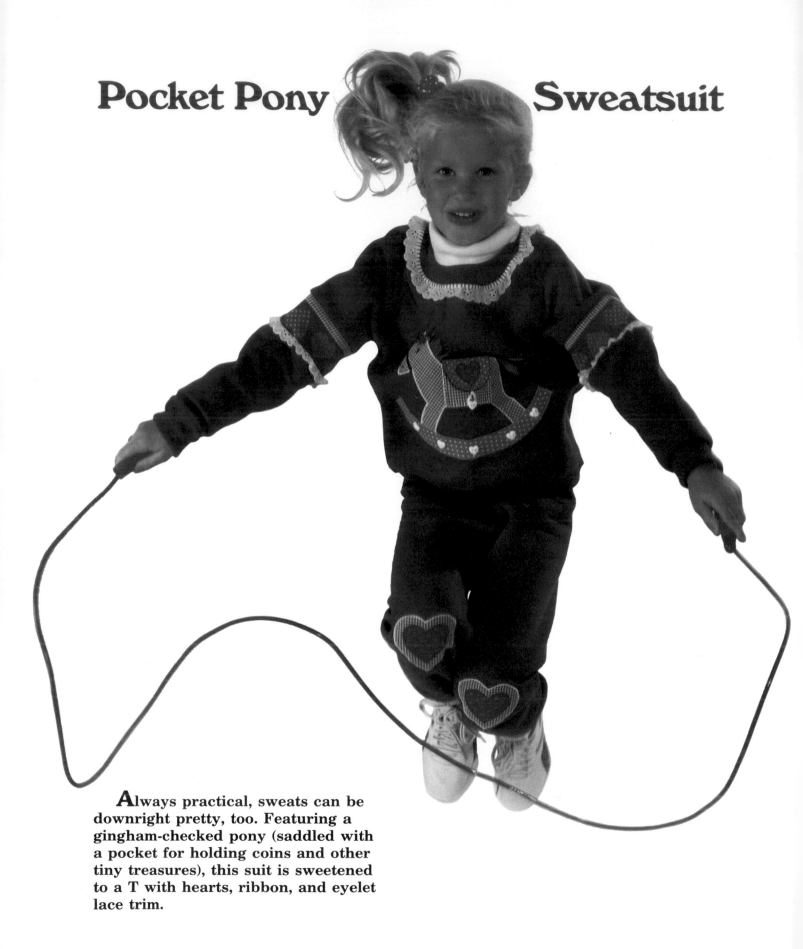

Always practical, sweats can be downright pretty, too. Featuring a gingham-checked pony (saddled with a pocket for holding coins and other tiny treasures), this suit is sweetened to a T with hearts, ribbon, and eyelet lace trim.

You will need:

Lavender sweatsuit
¼ yard (45″-wide) lavender checked fabric
8″ x 12″ piece of pink mini-heart print fabric
⅛ yard (36″-wide) large-heart print fabric
6″ x 8″ piece of red mini-print fabric
Thread (red, pink, white, and purple)
2½″ (⅛″-wide) white satin ribbon
¾ yard (⅛″-wide) red satin ribbon
2″ (⅛″-wide) dark purple satin ribbon
½ yard paper-backed fusible web
Lightweight paper (for stabilizing appliqué)
1½ to 1¾ yards (1″-wide) white gathered eyelet trim
6 (½″) white heart buttons
Red, white, and purple embroidery floss

Pony Appliqué

1. Cut pieces of web and fabric large enough for pony pattern. Trace pony pattern onto paper side of web; fuse web and fabric pieces. Repeat for rocker and pocket heart. Cut out appliqué pieces. Cut pocket flap as marked. From checked fabric, cut two 2½″ x 2¾″ rectangles for the pocket.

2. Remove paper backing from web on pocket heart and fuse heart to right side of one pocket flap. Pin a piece of paper to wrong side of flap. Appliqué heart, using red thread; tear away paper.

Loop white ribbon in half and tack ends to center of curved flap edge, with raw edges aligned and loop toward inside. Sew pocket flaps with right sides together, using ¼″ seam allowance and leaving straight edge open. Clip curves; turn and press flap. Blanket-stitch curved edge, using three strands of red floss.

3. Remove paper backing from web on pony and rocker; position pieces on sweatshirt and fuse lightly. Gently lift edge of pony's back and position straight edge of pocket flap so that ½″ lies under pony. From red ribbon, cut five 2″ pieces for mane and three 4½″ pieces for tail.

Loop ribbons in half and position cut ends under pony appliqué, as marked on pattern; press with tip of iron to secure. Press remainder of appliqué to secure. Cut a piece of paper large enough to back entire appliqué and pin to inside of shirt. Appliqué pony, using white thread; appliqué rocker with pink thread. Tear away paper and press appliqué.

4. With right sides together, stitch pocket pieces, using ¼″ seam allowance and leaving a 1″ opening along one side (2½″) edge. Clip corners and turn; slipstitch opening and press pocket. Sew side and bottom edges of pocket to pony, using three strands of white floss and blanket stitch.

5. Sew heart buttons to bottom edge of pocket and to rocker as marked (Xs). Embroider pony's face as marked, using three strands of purple floss for eye and nostril and two strands for eyelashes. Cut a piece of purple ribbon for the halter and sew to face, using blanket stitch. Tie a tiny red bow and tack between pony's ears.

Neck, Sleeve, and Knee Trim

1. Cut a piece of eyelet to fit around bottom edge of neck ribbing, adding 1″ extra for turning under ends. Sew straight edge of eyelet to edge of ribbing, using three strands of red floss and blanket stitch. Turn under ends of eyelet and whipstitch.

2. For sleeves, cut a 3″-wide band from each shirt sleeve. Open band seams by removing stitches. Measure top edge of one band and add 1″. Using this measurement for length, cut two 3⅜″-wide strips from large-heart fabric, two 1″-wide strips from checked fabric, and two pieces of eyelet.

3. Place right sleeve band with right side and top edge up. Place one heart fabric strip, right side up, along bottom edge of band and machine-baste strip to band.

With right sides together and edges aligned, stitch checked strip to heart strip, sewing through all three layers. Turn checked strip right side up and press lightly; machine-baste top edge to band. Sew strips to left sleeve band in same manner.

Trim excess fabric from strips. With right sides together, sew ends of bands back together. Finish seams with zigzag or overlock stitch.

4. Measure top edge of cut sleeve (bottom portion) and cut piece of eyelet to fit, adding ½″. With right sides together, baste eyelet to cut edge, turning under eyelet ends at seam; whipstitch ends. Sew bottom portion of sleeve to right sleeve

band, matching underarm seams and easing band to fit. Repeat for remaining sleeve.

Turn shirt inside out. With right sides together, sew bands back to shirt, matching underarm seams and easing to fit. Finish seams with zigzag or overlock stitch. Turn shirt right side out and press.

5. For knees, cut pieces of web and fabric large enough for large and small knee hearts. Trace hearts onto paper side of web. Fuse web and fabric pieces; cut out hearts.

6. Determine location of knees on pants. Remove inseam stitching at knees, making about a 10″ opening in each leg. Remove paper backing from web on hearts; position and fuse hearts. Cut a piece of paper large enough to back each large heart and pin to inside of pants. Appliqué large hearts, using white thread; appliqué small hearts with red thread. Tear away paper; press appliqués. Restitch inseam.

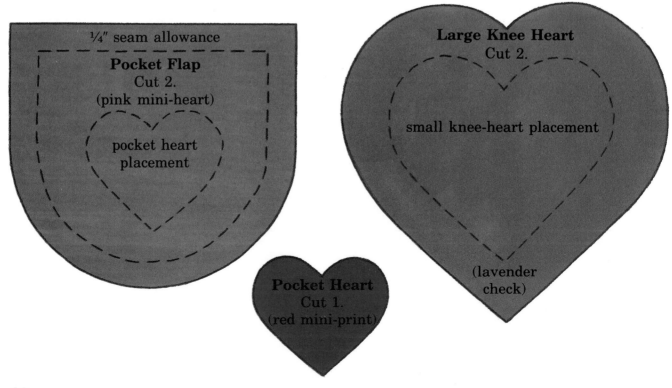

¼″ seam allowance

Pocket Flap
Cut 2.
(pink mini-heart)

pocket heart placement

Large Knee Heart
Cut 2.

small knee-heart placement

(lavender check)

Pocket Heart
Cut 1.
(red mini-print)

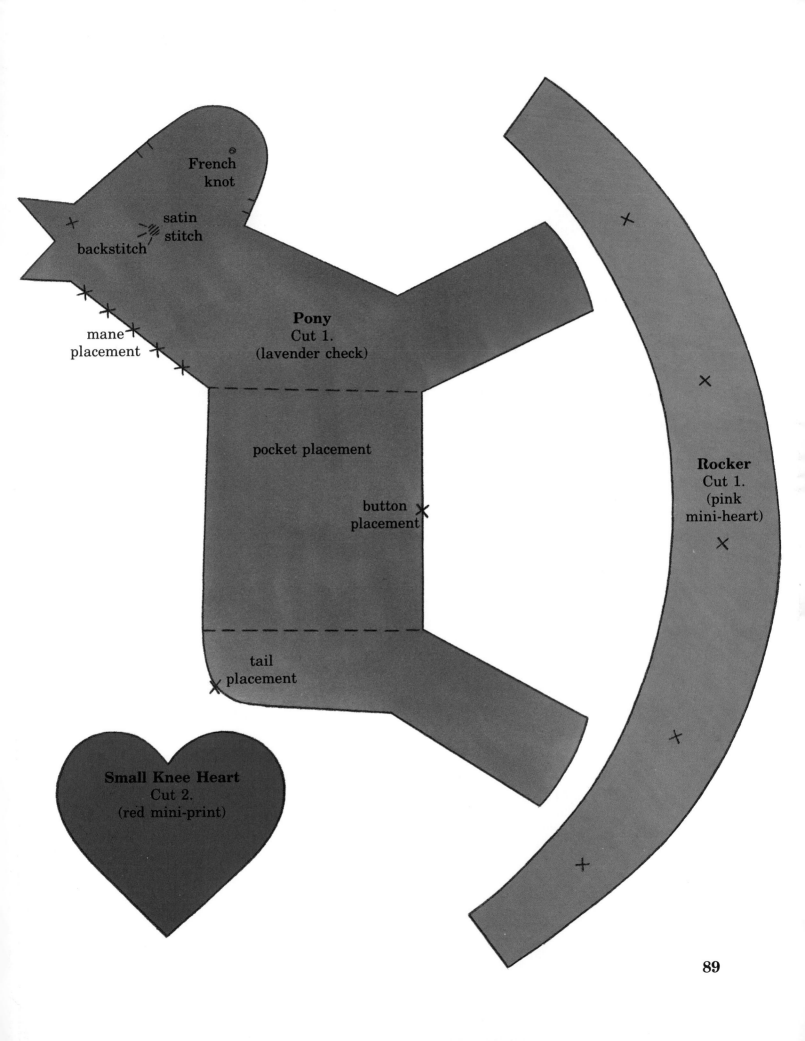

French
knot

satin
stitch

backstitch

mane
placement

Pony
Cut 1.
(lavender check)

pocket placement

button
placement

tail
placement

Small Knee Heart
Cut 2.
(red mini-print)

Rocker
Cut 1.
(pink
mini-heart)

Buttons 'n Bows

Dressed in bows from her head to her toes, a girl will look fashionable wherever she goes!

Headband
You will need:
2 yards (1½"-wide) solid ribbon
1 narrow headband
Clear tape
2 gold tips for headband
Water-soluble marking pen
1 yard (1½"-wide) plaid ribbon
Thin wire
4" (⅜"-wide) solid ribbon

1. Cut the two yards of 1½"-wide solid ribbon in half. Fold one piece of ribbon with long edges together; stitch, using a scant ⅛" seam allowance and leaving ends open. Gather ribbon onto headband and tightly wrap ends of ribbon with tape. Glue gold tips over taped ends, holding tips until dry.

2. Using the water-soluble pen, mark remaining piece of solid 1½"-wide ribbon at the following intervals: 4", 10½", 18½", 25½", and 33".

3. To make bow, place solid ribbon (marked side up) on top of plaid ribbon. Holding ribbons together as one, bring the 4" mark to the 10½" mark and pinch together to form center of bow. Bring the 18½" mark to center front of bow and pinch. Keeping plaid ribbon on the outside, bring the 25½" mark to center back and pinch. For final loop, bring the 33" mark to center front and pinch. Wrap center of bow securely with wire. Trim ends of ribbon.

4. Position bow on headband and wrap the ⅜" ribbon around the wire and headband. Glue ribbon to secure, trimming end if necessary. Let dry.

Shoestrings
You will need:
Pair of shoestrings
Ribbon (assorted widths and colors)
Thin wire
Hot-glue gun and glue stick

1. To make each bow, loop a ribbon (approximately 9½″ long) so that the ends overlap at center back. Pinch the center of the loop and wrap it tightly with a piece of wire.

2. Fold each shoestring in half to find center. Place center of a bow on center of a shoestring; wrap bow and shoestring with a piece of narrow ribbon, overlapping the ribbon ends. Glue ends; let dry.

Gloves
You will need:
Pair of knitted gloves
Ribbon (assorted widths and colors)
Thin wire
Hot-glue gun and glue stick
Buttons and rhinestones
Sewing needle and thread (optional)

Note: If gluing shank buttons to gloves, first remove shanks with wire cutters.

1. Make two matching ribbon bows, following step 1 for Shoestrings. (To make "double bows," use two widths of ribbon, placing narrower ribbon on top.)

2. Wrap a piece of narrow ribbon around the wire on each bow, overlapping the ribbon ends; glue to hold.

3. Glue bows to gloves. Glue or sew on buttons; glue rhinestones. Let dry.

Vest-Dressed

Better bone up on your appliqué. Once you spot these versatile designs, you'll be hounded by the itch to stitch!

You will need:
Garment to be appliquéd
Fabric scraps (refer to patterns for colors)
Thread to match
Lightweight fusible interfacing
Fusible web
For the Christmas Appliqué: 2 yards (⅜″-wide) red picot ribbon, small red heart button, 20 assorted Christmas buttons (or pins, bows, bells, etc.), tiny beads
For the Puppy Appliqué: buttons (2 for eyes, 1 butterfly, 3 bones, and 1 star), tiny bell, 2 (3½″) pieces of white jumbo rickrack

Note: Use medium-width satin stitch and matching thread to appliqué. Refer to photographs for placement of pieces.

Christmas Appliqué

1. Fuse pieces of interfacing to wrong side of scraps.

2. Enlarge alphabet appliqués to desired size on copy machine. Trace letters for name; cut one from fabric and one from web. Fuse letters to garment, following instructions of web manufacturer. Appliqué middle letter first; then appliqué one letter above it and one below, continuing until name is complete.

3. Cut holly leaves as marked and fuse to garment. Appliqué. Sew heart button between leaves for berry.

4. Cut pieces for appliqué as marked. Set star aside. Position stand, trunk, and tree sections (bottom, middle, top) on garment, in that order; fuse. Appliqué the pieces, beginning with top of tree and ending with stand. Fuse and appliqué the star.

Tack one end of ribbon to tree, at the top. Twist ribbon and arrange it in garland fashion; pin. Secure the ribbon at intervals by sewing on beads. Sew the Christmas buttons onto the tree.

Puppy Appliqué

1. Follow steps 1 and 2 for Christmas Appliqué.

2. Cut pieces for puppy and large bone as marked. Position pieces on garment, referring to pattern for order, and fuse. Appliqué puppy, stitching pieces in the following order: hind spot, main body/head, hind leg/tummy/foreleg, muzzle, nose, ears, tail, tongue, and collar. Sew on button eyes and butterfly button; sew bell to the collar. Fuse and appliqué the bone.

3. Cut pieces for doghouse, small bone, and shrubs as marked. Position pieces on garment, placing house on top of plaid doorway and tucking edge of rickrack under roof. Fuse and then appliqué pieces. Sew on star and bone buttons.

Alphabet Appliqués
For Holiday Appliqué, cut name from white mini-print and web.
For Puppy Appliqué, cut name from red pindot and web.

Patterns for Christmas Appliqué

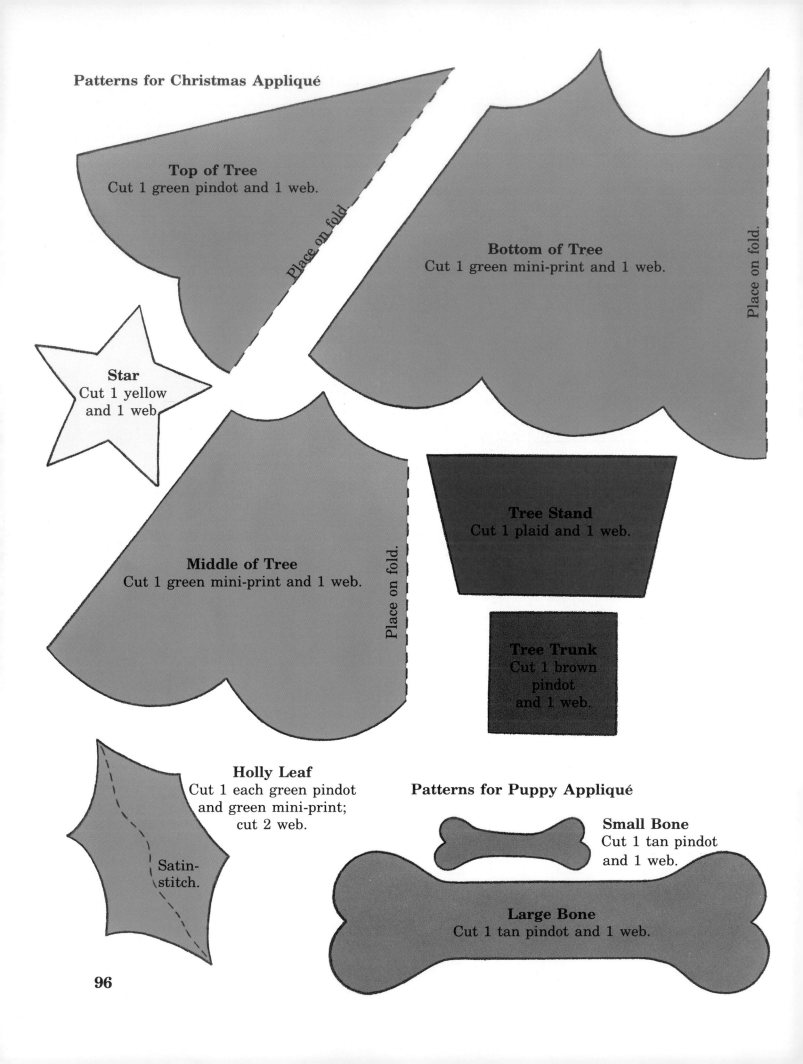

Top of Tree
Cut 1 green pindot and 1 web.

Place on fold.

Bottom of Tree
Cut 1 green mini-print and 1 web.

Place on fold.

Star
Cut 1 yellow
and 1 web.

Middle of Tree
Cut 1 green mini-print and 1 web.

Place on fold.

Tree Stand
Cut 1 plaid and 1 web.

Tree Trunk
Cut 1 brown
pindot
and 1 web.

Holly Leaf
Cut 1 each green pindot
and green mini-print;
cut 2 web.

Satin-
stitch.

Patterns for Puppy Appliqué

Small Bone
Cut 1 tan pindot
and 1 web.

Large Bone
Cut 1 tan pindot and 1 web.

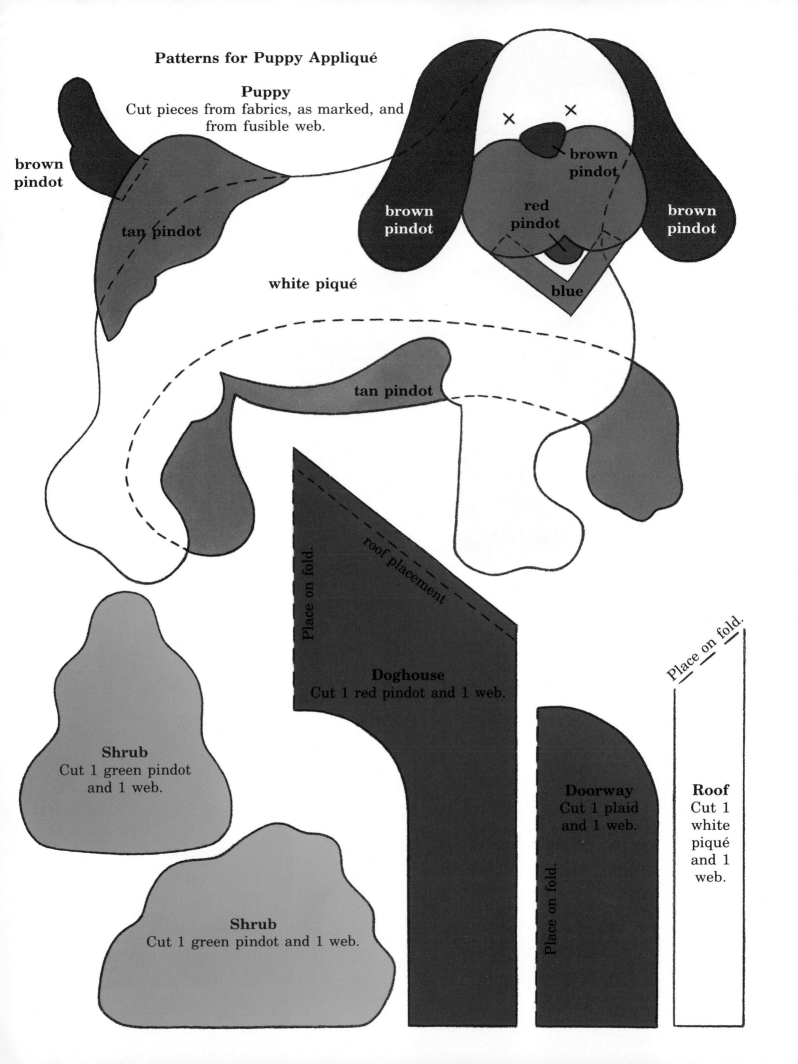

Patterns for Puppy Appliqué

Puppy
Cut pieces from fabrics, as marked, and from fusible web.

brown pindot

tan pindot

brown pindot

brown pindot

red pindot

brown pindot

blue

white piqué

tan pindot

Place on fold.

roof placement

Doghouse
Cut 1 red pindot and 1 web.

Shrub
Cut 1 green pindot and 1 web.

Shrub
Cut 1 green pindot and 1 web.

Doorway
Cut 1 plaid and 1 web.

Place on fold.

Place on fold.

Roof
Cut 1 white piqué and 1 web.

Santa Puzzle

Starring Santa, this puzzle will be fun for a tot (age three or older) to find in his stocking or under the tree. Cut from pine, it has five pieces and stands when assembled.

You will need:
Tracing paper
8″ x 9″ (¾″-thick) pine
Carbon paper
Scroll saw (or jigsaw)
Sandpaper
Paintbrushes (⅜″ flat and small round)
Acrylic paint (white, red, blue, yellow, green, and black)
Clear acrylic spray enamel

98

1. Trace complete pattern for puzzle. Cut out pattern, cutting along the outline.

2. Draw around the pattern on the pine. Using carbon paper and pencil, transfer the cutting lines (heavy black lines) for the puzzle pieces. Cut out the pieces with the scroll saw.

3. Sand fronts and backs of puzzle pieces. Sand outer edges of pieces that form outline of puzzle, slightly rounding the edges. Sand remaining edges lightly. (Do not round these.)

4. Spray pieces with clear acrylic. Let dry and sand lightly. Paint pieces white and let dry. Assemble puzzle. Using carbon paper and pencil, transfer details for painting. Spread out puzzle pieces; paint tops and edges, applying several coats and letting the paint dry between coats. Paint backs of pieces solid red. Let dry. Finish pieces with several coats of clear acrylic. Let dry.

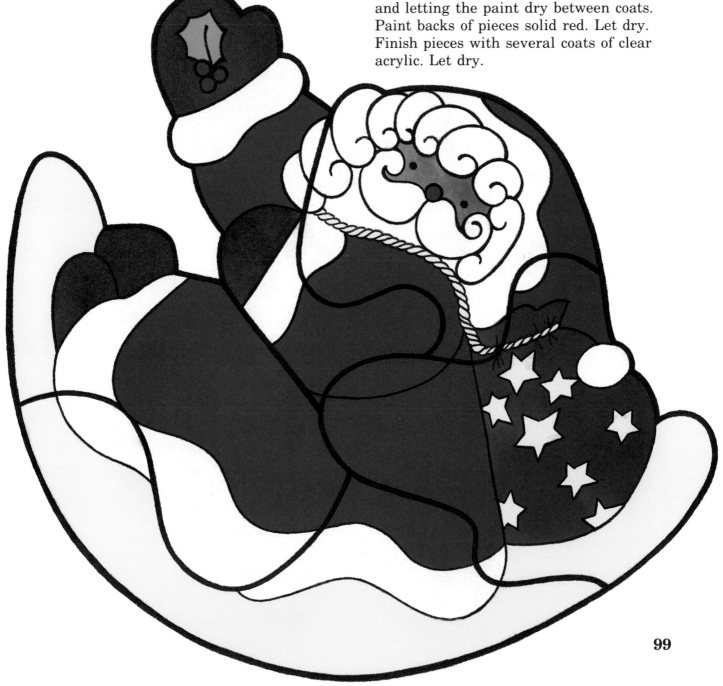

Sugarplum Fairy Wand

Absolutely doll-ing! A fluff of yellow hair, feathers and a bow, and a pink net tutu turn an impish face into a fairy fit for a wand.

You will need:

6″ x 7″ piece of pale pink fabric
Black fine-tip permanent marker
Polyester stuffing
22″ (⅜″-diameter) wooden dowel, painted
  white
Large yellow bead with ⅜″-diameter hole
Hot-glue gun and glue stick
Scrap of pink felt
Pink pom-pom (very small)
6 yards of yellow yarn
8″ x 36″ piece of pink-and-white print
  fabric
⅓ yard of pink netting
1½ yards (⅞″-wide) pink-and-white
  checked ribbon
2 white feathers
3 small gold bells
2 yards (⅜″-wide) pink-and-white checked
  ribbon
2 yards (⅜″-wide) white picot ribbon
Thread to match fabrics, yarn, and
  ribbons

Note: Use ¼″ seam allowance throughout.

1. Transfer pattern for doll and cut as
marked. Using marker, trace mouth and
eyes onto right side of one doll. With
right sides together and edges aligned,
sew doll pieces, leaving opening as
marked. Turn doll and stuff firmly. Turn
bottom edges under and slipstitch, leaving
½″ opening for dowel.

  Put glue on 4″ of dowel, at one end; insert dowel through opening. Stitch opening completely closed around dowel. Glue
bead onto other end of dowel. Cut cheeks
as marked and glue to face; glue on pom-
pom nose. Let dry.

2. To make hair, cut yarn into 18″
lengths. Wind a length around four fingers; slip loops off fingers, pinch center,
and hand-stitch to doll's head. Repeat so
that loops cover entire head.

3. To make skirt, fold print fabric in
half widthwise (short edges together),
with right sides together. Stitch edges.
Press seam open and turn skirt right side
out. With wrong sides together, fold skirt
in half lengthwise and press. Run a line
of gathering stitches along raw edges. Put
skirt on doll and gather to fit. Distribute
gathers evenly and secure. Hand-stitch
edge of skirt to doll.

4. To make tutu, cut netting into two 6″-
wide pieces. Fold one piece in half lengthwise and run a line of gathering stitches
along folded edge. Gather netting to 6″

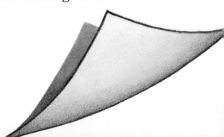

and secure. Repeat for remaining piece. Tack gathered edges of tutu pieces around doll, covering gathered edge of skirt.

5. Cut a 36″ piece of ⅞″-wide ribbon and tack to center front of the tutu, skirt, and doll; continue tacking at 2″ intervals, leaving ribbon loose between tacks. (See figure.) Tie ribbon ends into a bow at back.

6. Tie remaining piece of ⅞″-wide ribbon into a bow; sew to head. Glue ends of feathers behind bow; tack a bell to center of bow. Let dry.

7. To make streamers, fold remaining ribbons in half; fold ribbons again, 5″ from folds. Tack entire bundle of ribbons to doll at dowel, so that 5″ loops hang in front. Tie remaining bells onto two ribbon ends.

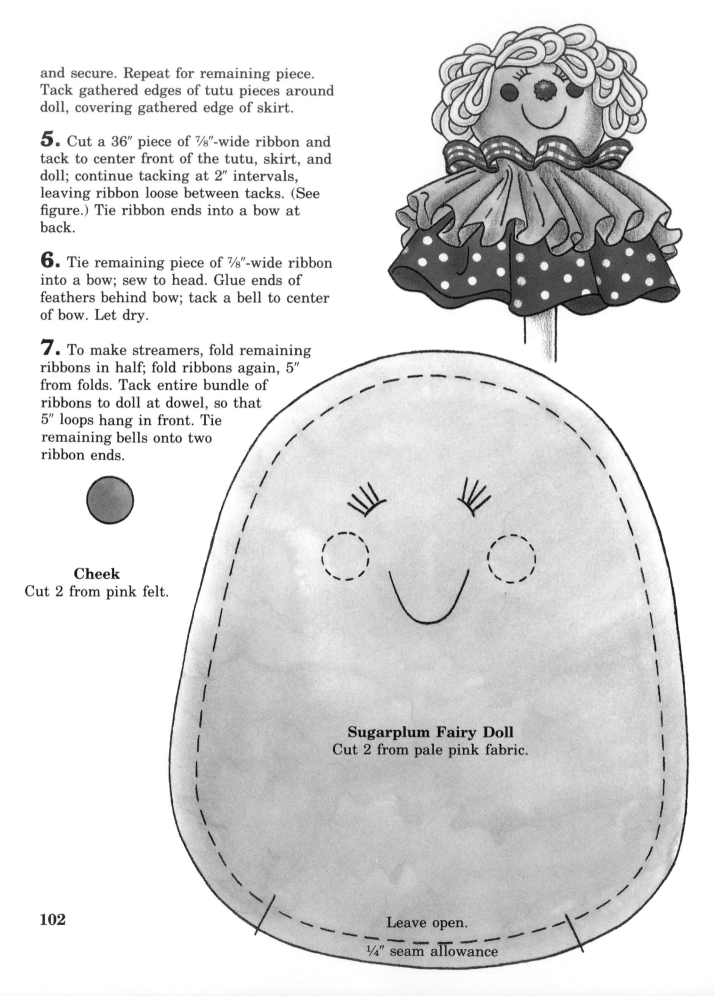

Cheek
Cut 2 from pink felt.

Sugarplum Fairy Doll
Cut 2 from pale pink fabric.

102

Leave open.

¼″ seam allowance

Goodnight, Barrettes

She'll know where to find her barrettes every morning if they're clipped onto these ribbon moonbeams at night.

You will need:
Tracing paper
⅓ yard (45″-wide) yellow cotton fabric
12″ x 14″ piece of quilt batting
¼ yard (36″-wide) blue dotted swiss
Thread to match fabrics
Dressmakers' carbon
Polyester stuffing
1¼ yards (1″-wide) pink grosgrain ribbon
Paintbrush
Acrylic paint (blue, brown, pink, and white)
Black fine-tip permanent marker
½ yard (⅛″-wide) pink satin ribbon

1. Trace the patterns for the moon (including facial features) and star. Cut pieces as marked. Using dressmakers' carbon, lightly transfer facial features to right side of one yellow moon.

2. Pin the batting moon to wrong side of moon face. On right side of moon face, machine-sew along facial features, using yellow thread and stitching through both thicknesses. Cut slits in batting at eyebrow, cheek, and mouth; stuff lightly and sew openings closed.

3. Pin moon face to moon back with right sides together. Sew, leaving opening as marked. Trim seams and clip curves; turn moon and stuff.

4. Cut the grosgrain ribbon into three 15″ lengths. Cut one end of each 15″ ribbon at an angle. With ribbons placed side by side, tuck straight ends inside opening in moon. Hand-sew opening closed with ribbon ends inside, using double thread and tiny stitches.

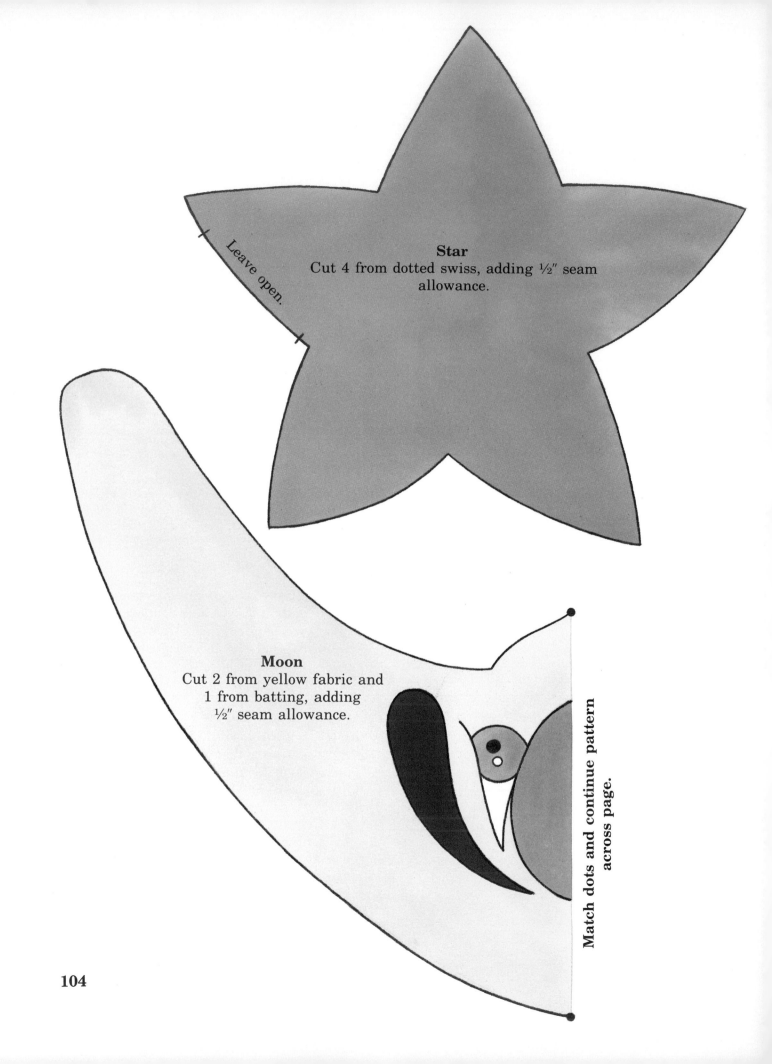

Star
Cut 4 from dotted swiss, adding ½″ seam allowance.

Leave open.

Moon
Cut 2 from yellow fabric and 1 from batting, adding ½″ seam allowance.

Match dots and continue pattern across page.

5. Pin stars with right sides together and sew, leaving opening in each as marked. Trim seams and clip curves. Turn, press, and stuff stars; sew openings closed.

6. Paint moon face, referring to pattern for colors. (Use marker to paint black on eye.) Let dry.

7. Arrange stars and tack to moon. Tack stars together. To form loop for hanging moon, sew ends of satin ribbon to top of upper star.

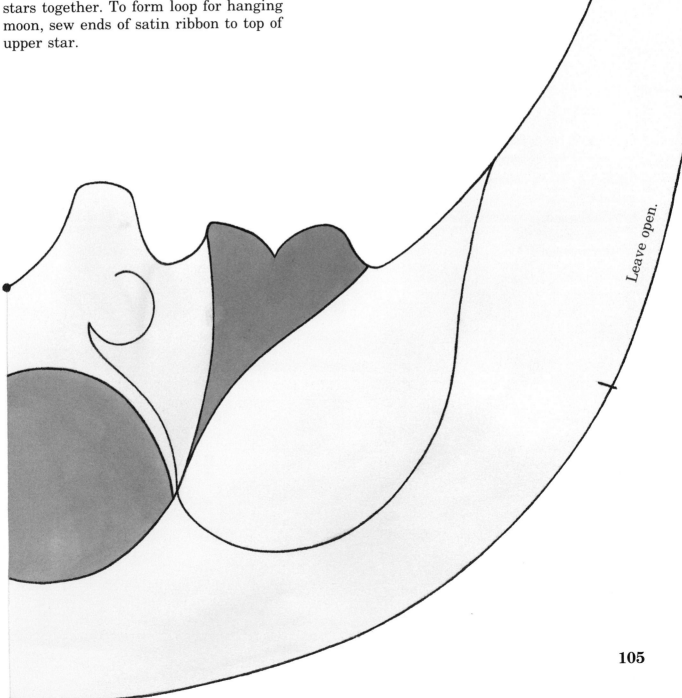

Leave open.

Kangaroo Camp Kit

When it comes to organization, who doesn't need a little help? Made like a shoebag, this handy kit has designated pockets for soap, shampoo, and other items that kids need to keep tidy at camp.

You will need:

2 yards (45″-wide) blue-and-black
    polka-dot fabric
9″ square of yellow fabric
9″ square of fusible web
Thread to match fabrics
19″ x 26″ piece of batting
⅔ yard (¼″-wide) elastic
Embroidery floss (for kangaroo's eye)
White colored pencil (or water-soluble
    fabric marker)
Large piece of heavy plastic
Paintbrushes
Acrylic paint (white, peach, and pink)
4″ x 5½″ mirror
2 (17¼″-long and ⅜″-diameter) wooden
    dowels

Cutting the Pieces

From the polka-dot fabric, cut the following pieces: two 19″ x 26″ rectangles (kit front and backing), one 1″ x 24″ strip (mirror straps), one 9½″ x 27″ rectangle (top pocket strip), one 9½″ x 25″ rectangle (bottom pocket strip), five yards of 2″-wide bias binding, and two ½″ x 24½″ strips (ties).

Kangaroo Appliqué

1. Cut kangaroo and pocket as marked. For kangaroo arm, cut two 3″ squares from yellow fabric and one 3″ square from fusible web; fuse fabric squares. Transfer arm pattern to fused square.

2. Lay one 19″ x 26″ polka-dot rectangle right side up, with 19″ edge at top. (This will be kit front.) With fabric piece on top of fusible web piece, position kangaroo so that ears are ⅝″ below top edge of kit front and tail is 3″ from left-hand edge. Fuse kangaroo, following instructions of web manufacturer.

3. Turn top edge of kangaroo pocket to wrong side ¼″ and press; turn edge again ½″ and press. Cut a 1″ length of elastic and zigzag it to pocket along second fold, stretching the elastic as you sew. Pin pocket to kangaroo, with wrong side of pocket to right side of kangaroo; baste side and bottom edges, gathering bottom edge of pocket to fit. Appliqué pocket (side and bottom edges) to kangaroo and kangaroo to kit front, using matching thread and satin stitch; stitch again, using a slightly wider stitch.

4. Satin-stitch arm outline on fabric square, stitching from dot to dot as marked on pattern. Cut out arm; stitch edges again. Appliqué raw edges of arm to kangaroo; stitch again.

5. Using three strands of floss and three wraps, make a French knot for the kangaroo's eye.

Mirror Straps and Pockets

1. To make the mirror straps, cut a 12″ length of elastic. Lay the 1″ x 24″ polka-dot strip wrong side up. Fold one long edge of the strip ¼″ toward center and press; position elastic inside fold. Fold opposite long edge ⅛″ toward center and press; fold edge again ¼″ and press. Zigzag strip, stretching the elastic to fit strip. Cut the strip in half.

2. On right side of kit front, make a mark 3½″ from the right-hand side and the top edge; make another mark approximately 2″ below the first mark. Zigzag ends of one mirror strap to kit front at these marks; zigzag ends of second strap 3½″ to left of first strap.

Figure A

Top Pocket Strip

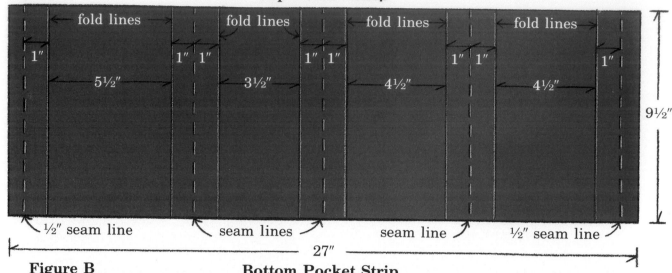

fold lines   fold lines   fold lines   fold lines

1"   1" 1"   1" 1"   1" 1"   1"

5½"   3½"   4½"   4½"

9½"

½" seam line   seam lines   seam line   ½" seam line

27"

Figure B

Bottom Pocket Strip

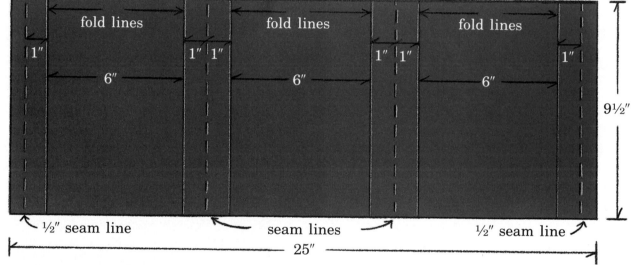

fold lines   fold lines   fold lines

1"   1" 1"   1" 1"   1"

6"   6"   6"

9½"

½" seam line   seam lines   ½" seam line

25"

Figure C

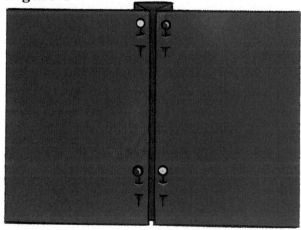

3. Turn one long edge of the top pocket strip ½" to the wrong side; turn edge ½" again and press. Topstitch close to edge of the second fold. Repeat for the bottom pocket strip.

4. Using the white pencil, mark seam and vertical fold lines on top and bottom pocket strips. (Figures A and B.)

5. On each pocket strip, fold and press all fold lines with wrong sides together. Lay strips right side up. To form pleats, bring the pressed fold lines to the marked seam lines and pin (Figure C); press. Machine-baste strips ⅜" from bottom edges.

6. Transfer design patterns to pockets, referring to photograph for placement. To protect kit front from paint, cut pieces of plastic to fit inside pockets. Base-coat shapes white and let dry. Paint the shapes, referring to patterns for colors. Let dry.

7. Using the white pencil, draw horizontal lines across right side of kit front, 2″ and 10″ up from bottom edge. Lay bottom pocket strip (right side down) on kit front, aligning bottom edge of strip with 2″ line; pin, adjusting pleats. Sew strip to kit front, using ½″ seam allowance. Repeat for top pocket strip, aligning bottom edge of strip with 10″ line on kit front.

8. Turn pockets up and press. With raw edges aligned, baste ends of pocket strips to side edges of kit front, using ¼″ seam allowance.

Finishing the Kit

1. Satin-stitch child's name 1″ above mirror straps, if desired.

2. Place batting rectangle on top of kit backing (r ght side down) and center kit front (right side up) on top. Pin the three layers together along the outer edges and vertical seam lines. To keep batting from shifting, hand-baste layers securely.

3. Machine-quilt kit, stitching beneath both rows of pockets and above top row, and being careful not to sew pockets closed. Remove pins and quilt down the seam line in center of each pleat, backstitching at ends to secure. Quilt around outline of kangaroo. Center mirror in elastic straps and draw around mirror. Remove the mirror and quilt along the outline.

4. Make a continuous bias strip for the binding. With raw edges aligned and right sides together, pin binding along outer edges of the kit, beginning and ending at center bottom edge; machine-stitch, using ½″ seam allowance.

5. Trim batting and kit backing to match raw edges of kit front. Fold binding to back of kit. Tuck under raw edge of binding to cover stitching line; blindstitch, leaving 1½″ openings at lower left and upper right corners. Slide dowels into openings; blindstitch openings closed.

6. Fold each tie strip in half with long edges and right sides together; sew raw edges, using ½″ seam allowance and leaving ends open. Turn ties right side out and press. Turn raw edges in ¼″; handstitch ties securely to upper corners of kit.

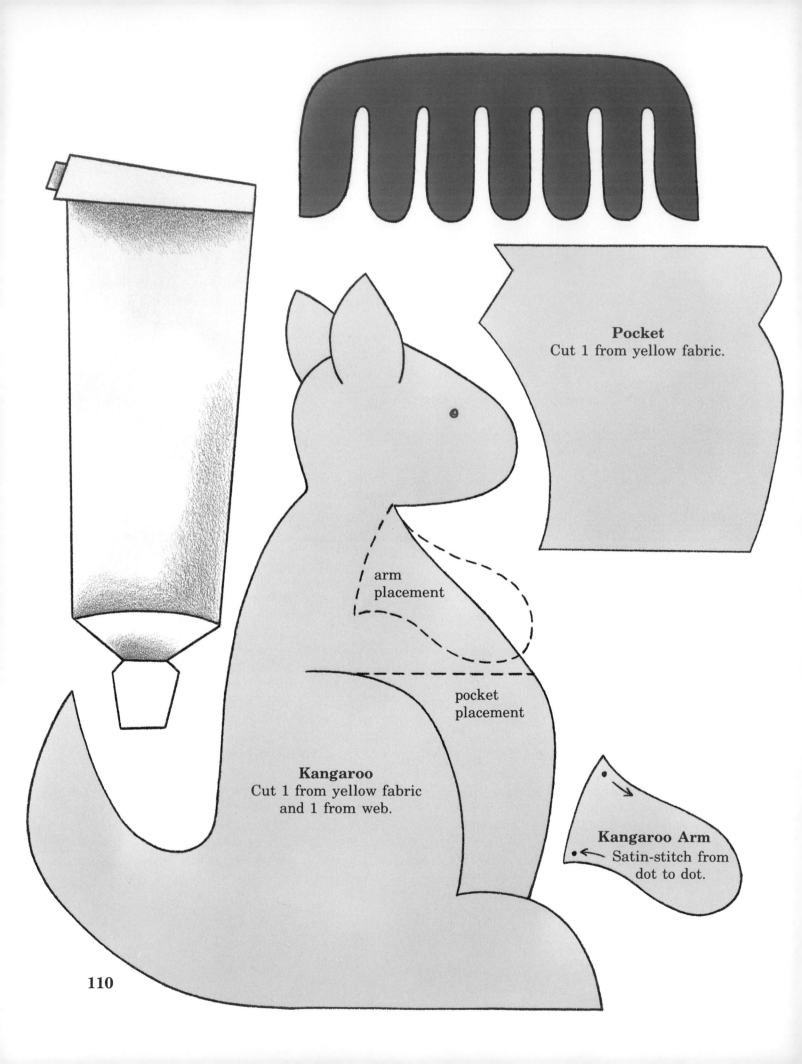

Pocket
Cut 1 from yellow fabric.

arm
placement

pocket
placement

Kangaroo
Cut 1 from yellow fabric
and 1 from web.

Kangaroo Arm
Satin-stitch from
dot to dot.

110

Teddy Peg Rack

"**B**earied" under mountains of mittens and scarves? Provide this fellow with a place to park, and your children will be charmed to hang up their clothes.

You will need:
Tracing and graphite paper
10″ x 14″ (¾″-thick) best-grade fir
Band saw (or jigsaw)
5″ x 12″ (¼″-thick) plywood
Scroll saw
Sandpaper
2 (3½″-long) wooden pegs
Electric drill with ³⁄₆₄″ bit
Acrylic paint (white, red, light tan, silver, black, bright yellow, turquoise)
Stencil plastic
Ballpoint pen
Craft knife
Stencil adhesive
Stencil brushes
Paintbrushes (½″ and fine-tipped)
Masking tape
Clear acrylic spray enamel
Wood glue
2 (1½″-long) #6 flat-head wood screws
Sawtooth picture hanger

Note: Use stencil brushes and stenciling technique (up-and-down dabbing motion) to paint all pieces, except pegs, on front of peg rack. When changing colors, use a clean, dry brush. Use the ½″ brush and regular paint strokes to apply base coat and to paint pegs and edges of pieces.

1. Trace patterns (including features) for bear head, bear body/car, and bumper. Cut out the three patterns and piece them together, on top of a piece of tracing paper, to make one complete bear/car pattern. Draw around the outline of the bear/car pattern on the tracing paper. Reverse and transfer it to back of the fir. Cut out the bear/car, using the band saw. Transfer patterns for arm and wheels to back of plywood; cut pieces as marked, using the scroll saw.

2. Sand all wood surfaces smooth, slightly rounding the edges. Mark placement for holes on the wheels and bumper.

3. Cut 1½″ off bottom end of pegs, using the scroll saw. Using the electric drill and ³/₆₄″ bit, center and drill a ½″-deep hole in bottom end of each peg; drill holes through the wheels and bumper.

4. Base-coat all pieces with several coats of white paint. Let dry. Paint pegs bright yellow and let dry.

5. Using graphite paper, transfer features to bear/car. Trace the following features from bear/car onto separate pieces of stencil plastic, using the ballpoint pen: hat, facial features, scarf, scarf squares, steering wheel, and car. Cut stencils with craft knife, reserving car (cut from stencil) for later use. Cut stencil for paw markings and cut hubcaps as marked.

6. Stencil car red (heavy coverage) and let dry. Spray back of reserved plastic car with adhesive and place on stenciled car. Using light tan paint (light coverage), paint portion of bear/car that is above car line (all of bear, scarf, and steering wheel). Paint arm light tan; paint bumper and wheels silver. Stencil scarf turquoise. Let dry.

Using black paint, stencil the hat, facial features, scarf squares, steering wheel, and paw markings. Spray plastic hubcaps with adhesive and center hubcaps on wheels; paint the wheels black. Let the paint dry.

7. Remove plastic car and hubcaps. Paint edges of bear/car, arm, and wheels, using masking tape to seal off areas that you are not working on. Let dry. Using white paint and fine-tipped brush, paint stitching lines on hat and fringe on scarf. Let dry.

8. Apply several coats of clear acrylic to all surfaces. Let dry.

9. Attach hanger to back of bear's head, positioning hanger off-center as shown. Center pegs over wheels and position wheels on car. From back of car, insert screws through holes and tighten securely. Glue arm in place and let dry.

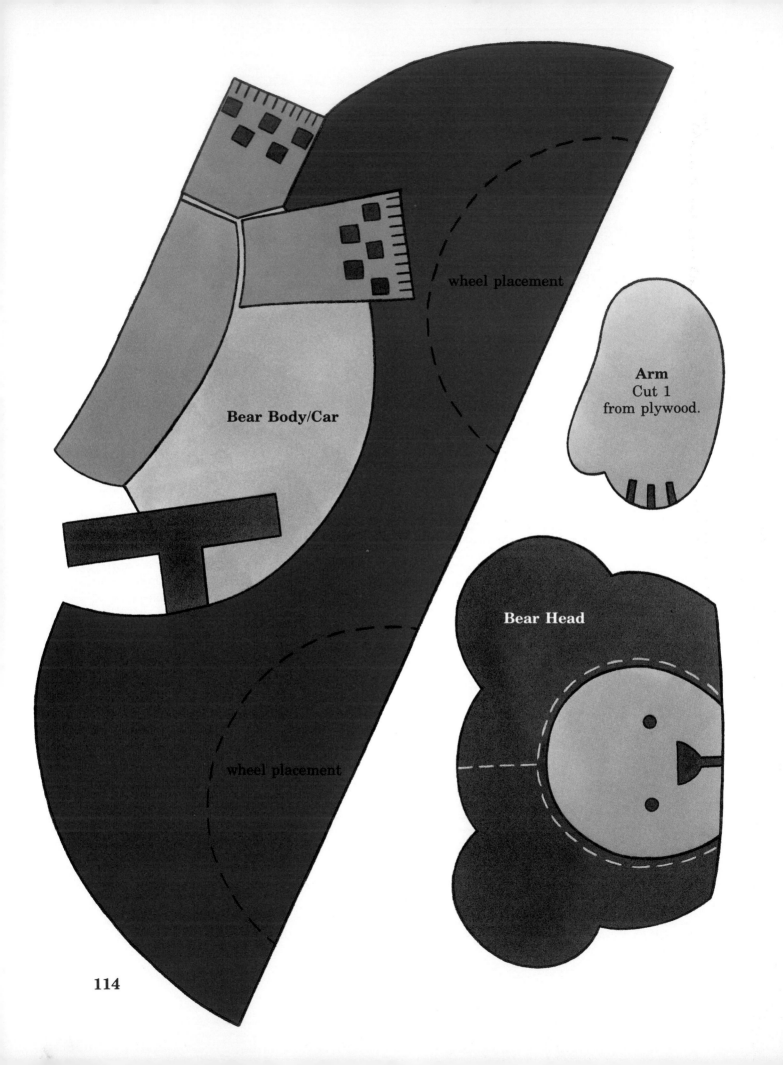

Arm
Cut 1
from plywood.

Bear Body/Car

wheel placement

wheel placement

Bear Head

114

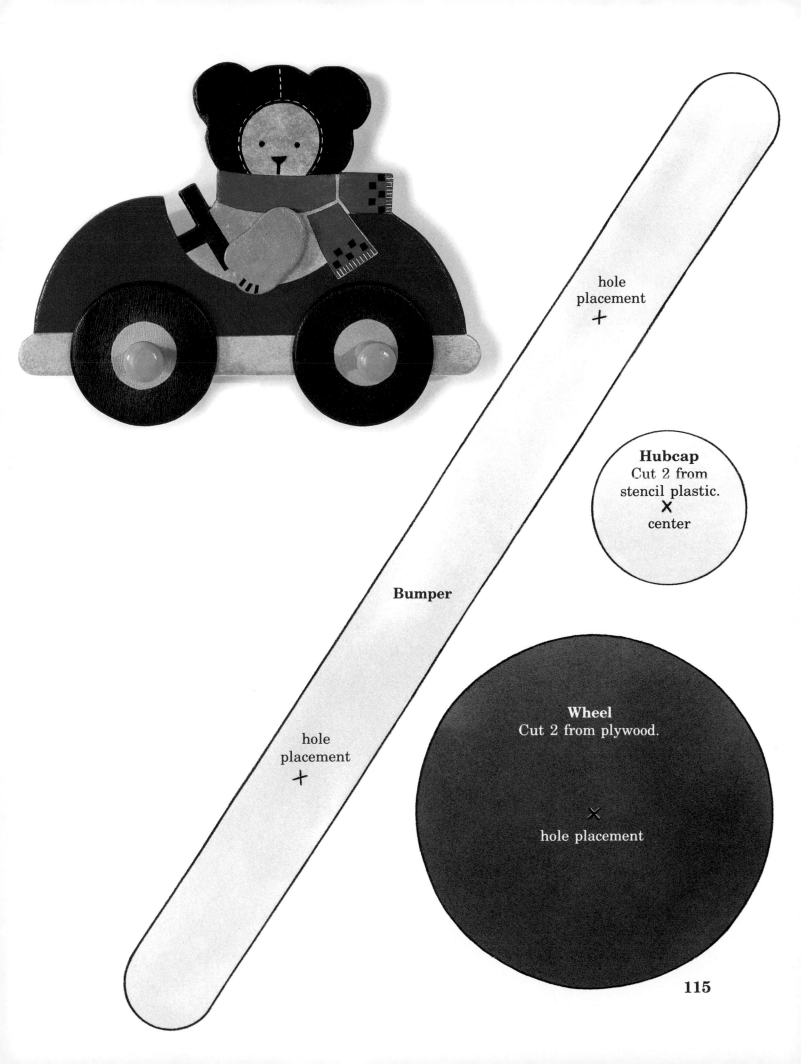

hole
placement

+

Bumper

hole
placement

+

Hubcap
Cut 2 from
stencil plastic.
✗
center

Wheel
Cut 2 from plywood.

✗

hole placement

115

Honey Bunny

Fashioned to help a young lady
get dressed, Honey's a perfectly
beautiful bunny-in-waiting!

You will need:

¼ yard (45″-wide) mini-print fabric for pocket

½ yard (45″-wide) tattersall check for body and base

4½″ x 16″ strip of floral-print fabric for arms

4½″ x 14″ strip of white cotton fabric for face and hands

Thread to match

¾ yard of narrow elastic cording

Drawing compass

Corrugated cardboard

9″-long cardboard tube

Hot-glue gun and glue stick

Polyester stuffing

¾ yard (1¼″-wide) gathered eyelet trim

Embroidery needle

Gray and pink embroidery floss

Pink colored pencil

White handkerchief with scalloped edges and embroidered corner

½ yard (⅛″-wide) pink satin ribbon

Straw hat to fit 2″ doll's head

¼ yard (⅜″-wide) print satin ribbon

1⅓ yards (⅛″-wide) white satin ribbon

4 purchased pink satin roses

Note: Use ¼″ seam allowance throughout project unless instructed otherwise.

Making Honey Bunny

1. To make shirred pocket, cut a 6⅝″ x 45″ strip of mini-print fabric. Fold in half lengthwise (long edges together) and press. Fold in half and press again, two times, to make seven creases. Unfold pocket piece. Finish one long edge with ⅜″ hem.

Lay elastic cording on wrong side of pocket piece, along crease closest to hemmed edge; securely stitch one end of cording to edge of fabric. Using widest zigzag stitch, sew over cording without catching it, stretching the cording as you sew. Stitch remaining end of cording to fabric to secure. Adjust gathers evenly.

Run lines of gathering stitches along remaining creases. Gather pocket to 27″; stitch along creases to secure gathers.

2. For body, cut an 11½″ x 27″ piece of tattersall check. Lay pocket on body piece, right sides up, and align bottom edges; baste pocket to body, stitching down one side, across last row of shirring, and up other side. At bottom of body/pocket, run a line of gathering stitches ¼″ from edge, beginning and ending ¼″ from sides; repeat gathering stitches ¼″ from top edge of body.

Tack center front of pocket to body at elastic cording. Measure 6¾″ from center front, first to one side and then the other,

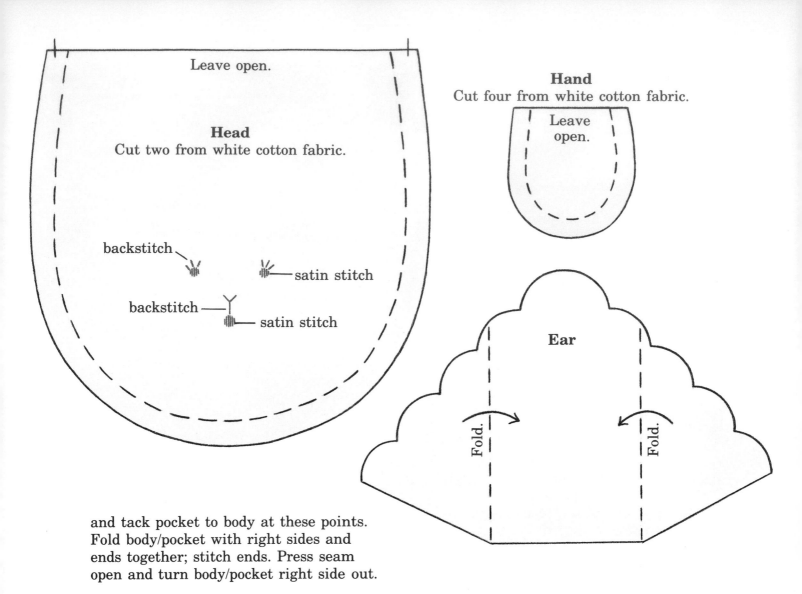

Head
Cut two from white cotton fabric.

Leave open.

backstitch

satin stitch

backstitch

satin stitch

Hand
Cut four from white cotton fabric.

Leave open.

Ear

Fold.

Fold.

and tack pocket to body at these points. Fold body/pocket with right sides and ends together; stitch ends. Press seam open and turn body/pocket right side out.

3. For bases, cut two 8½″ circles from cardboard. Slightly gather bottom edges of body/pocket. Slip one base into top of body and adjust so that edge of base runs along bottom row of shirring. Glue base to fabric to secure.

Glue one end of cardboard tube to center of base inside body. Stuff body lightly with polyester stuffing and slightly gather top edge. Put glue around top edge of tube. Quickly and tightly gather top edge of body to fit tube; knot threads to secure.

Cut one 9½″ circle from the tattersall check. Run a line of gathering stitches around fabric circle, ¼″ and then ½″ from edge. Lay remaining cardboard base on wrong side of fabric circle and pull threads tightly to gather around base; knot to secure.

Glue straight edge of eyelet to wrong side of base, along edge, so that scalloped edge of eyelet extends beyond base. Apply glue to wrong side of base and center bunny's body on top, with ends of eyelet and body seam in back. Hold body in place until glue is set.

4. Cut pieces for head as marked and transfer facial features to one piece. Using satin stitch and two strands of floss, embroider eyes gray and mouth pink. Backstitch eyelashes and nose with one strand of gray floss. Lightly color cheeks with pink pencil.

With right sides together, stitch head pieces, leaving straight edges open. Clip curves; turn head and stuff firmly. Gather top of head to close opening and secure.

118

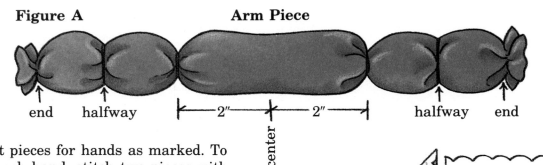

Figure A   **Arm Piece**

end   halfway   ⊢—2″—⊢—2″—⊣   halfway   end

center

5. Cut pieces for hands as marked. To make each hand, stitch two pieces with right sides together, leaving straight edges open. Clip curves; turn hand and stuff firmly. Gather straight edges to close; knot securely.

6. To make arms, stitch a narrow hem at each end of the floral-print strip. Then run a row of gathering stitches ¾″ from each end, starting and ending ¼″ from long edges. Fold arm piece in half length-wise, right sides together, and stitch long edges. Turn and stuff lightly.

Gather ends to close openings; knot. Tightly wrap arm piece with thread, 2″ on either side of center; knot to secure. Wrap thread loosely around arm piece, halfway between first wraps and ends; knot to secure. (Figure A.)

7. For collar, fold embroidered corner of handkerchief 3¼″ toward center, with wrong sides together; press. Cut off corner as shown. (Figure B.) Open corner and trim ¼″ off cut edges. Refold corner and sew a line of gathering stitches along the fold as shown. (Figure C.)

8. For ears, heavily starch remaining piece of handkerchief. Using pattern (for size), cut an ear from each of two remaining corners of handkerchief. Fold ears as marked and stitch bottom edges to secure.

Assembling Honey Bunny

1. Glue head to top of body. Place collar around bunny's neck and gather to fit; knot to secure. Tack collar ends to back of head. Tie pink ribbon around neck and make a bow in front; trim ends to desired length.

Figure B

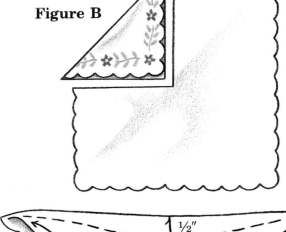

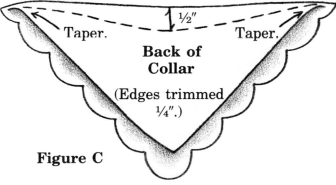

Taper.   ½″   Taper.

Back of Collar

(Edges trimmed ¼″.)

Figure C

2. Glue hands inside gathered ends of arm piece. Glue center of arm piece to back of head and body; hold until glue dries. Glue tips of hands together, using small amount of glue. Hold until dry.

3. Fold ears in half lengthwise and glue to sides of hat, with folds toward back. Cut print ribbon to fit around crown of hat, plus ½″. Glue ribbon to hat, covering bottom of ears. Apply glue to top of bunny's head and attach hat.

4. Cut four 12″ lengths of white ribbon. Tie bows and glue to pocket at points of tacking. Glue a rose to center of each bow. Let dry. Trim ribbon ends.

Crocodile Crunch

Ready to take a bite out of the toughest assignment, these crocs look cool cruising to school. Please note that the instructions that follow are for making the clipboard (the small croc with the snappy stripes).

You will need:
⅓ yard (45″-wide) green fabric
Thread to match
12″ square of fleece
Scraps of gold and blue felt
Embroidery floss to match blue felt
Poster paper
Clipboard with 6″ clip
Glue stick
Water-soluble marking pen
2 (⅝″-diameter) wiggly eyes

Note: Use ¼″ seam allowance throughout project unless instructed otherwise.

1. Transfer patterns to fabrics and cut as marked. Cut poster paper faces; glue together and let dry.

2. Draw around clipboard twice on green fabric; cut out the pieces, adding ½″ all around. Draw around clipboard on poster paper; cut out the piece, cutting it ¼″ smaller all around.

Fit one piece of fabric to front of clipboard, clipping corners and trimming fabric to fit around clip. Glue fabric to clipboard, smoothing fabric from center out and gluing excess to back. Glue remaining piece of fabric to poster paper, in same manner. Place fabric-covered poster paper under heavy object until dry.

3. Pin fleece face to wrong side of one fabric face. Using three strands of floss and outline stitch, embroider face wrinkles on front of face as marked on pattern. Glue nostrils in place and let dry.

4. Pin teeth to right side of face front as shown. (Figure A.) With right sides together, sew face front to face back, leaving opening as marked. Trim fleece and clip curves. Turn face right side out (teeth will now protrude); press. Slightly bow poster paper face and slide it through

Figure A

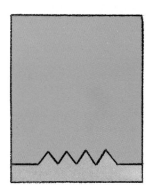

Figure B

opening; blindstitch opening closed. Sew wiggly eyes securely to face.

5. Position set of claws on right side of one fabric leg as shown. (Figure B.) Layer fleece leg, leg with claw (right side up), and plain fabric leg (right side down); stitch, leaving openings as marked. Trim fleece and corners; turn leg and press (claws will now protrude). Repeat for second leg, leaving openings as marked.

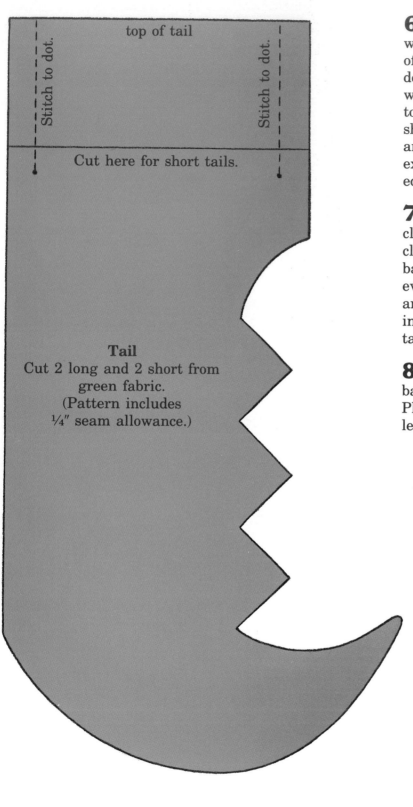

Tail
Cut 2 long and 2 short from
green fabric.
(Pattern includes
¼″ seam allowance.)

top of tail

Stitch to dot.

Stitch to dot.

Cut here for short tails.

6. To make tail pocket, place long tails with right sides together; stitch from top of tails to dots as marked. Clip seams at dots; turn and press tail. Place short tails with right sides together and sew along top edge; turn and press. Pin long and short tails together, aligning tips of tails and points. Stitch all around short tail, except top. Trim seam and zigzag raw edges. Turn tail pocket right side out.

7. Slide legs into place on either side of clip. Fold top raw edges of legs to back of clipboard and glue. Glue top of tail to back of clipboard so that edge of pocket is even with top of clipboard and tail points are toward clip. Sew face to clip, positioning bottom of face slightly below claws; tack underside of face to legs.

8. Glue fabric-covered poster paper to back of clipboard, covering all raw edges. Place clipboard under heavy object and let dry.

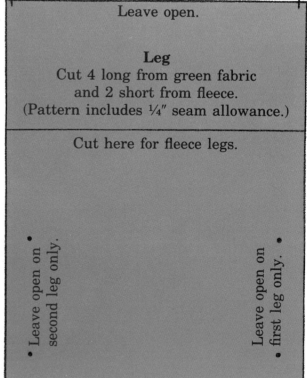

Leave open.

Leg
Cut 4 long from green fabric
and 2 short from fleece.
(Pattern includes ¼″ seam allowance.)

Cut here for fleece legs.

Leave open on second leg only.

Leave open on first leg only.

122

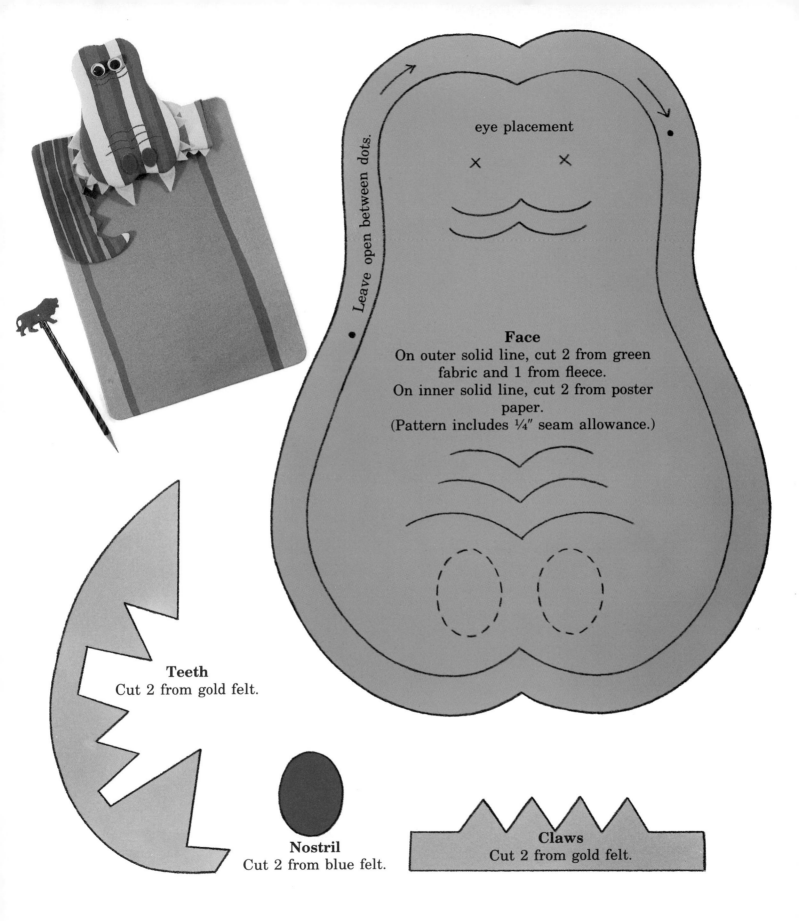

Face
On outer solid line, cut 2 from green fabric and 1 from fleece.
On inner solid line, cut 2 from poster paper.
(Pattern includes ¼″ seam allowance.)

eye placement

Leave open between dots.

Teeth
Cut 2 from gold felt.

Nostril
Cut 2 from blue felt.

Claws
Cut 2 from gold felt.

Dear Dolly Hangers

Glue simple-to-sew faces to fabric-covered hangers for a gift set that's frilly—and functional, too!

You will need (for each cover):
¼ yard (45"-wide) fabric
3 yards (½"-wide) white flat lace
Safety pin and 5" scrap of ribbon
Molded-plastic hanger (child size)
Coping saw
Hot-glue gun and glue stick
3" x 6" scrap of muslin
Thread to match fabrics and yarn
Polyester stuffing
Water-soluble marking pen
Permanent razor-point pens (or
   paintbrush and acrylic paint) for face
Pink colored pencil
Yarn for hair
Narrow ribbon for bows
3" (⅝"-wide) gathered eyelet trim
Small bell or novelty button

Note: Use ⅛" seam allowance throughout project unless instructed otherwise.

1. Cut fabric into two 2½″ x 45″ strips and one 2½″ x 18″ strip. Stitch to make one continuous strip. On right side of strips, baste straight edge of lace along one raw edge, with lace toward strip. Fold strip with right sides and long edges together and stitch, leaving one end open and stopping 3″ short of other end.

2. Attach safety pin to one end of the 5″ ribbon. Thread this end of ribbon into fabric tube so that other end of ribbon aligns with raw edges at end of tube; pin ribbon end at end of tube as shown. (Figure A.) Finish stitching side of tube and then stitch across end, catching ribbon end in stitching. Push safety pin to open end of tube, turning tube right side out. Cut off the ribbon.

3. Using the coping saw, cut through hanger as shown. (Figure B.) Starting at hook end, thread fabric tube onto hanger, adjusting tube so that lace faces outward. Make a 1″ slit in tube at point of cut on hanger. Glue cut edges of hanger back together and let dry completely. Hand-stitch openings in tube to close.

4. Fold muslin with ends together, making a 3″ square. Transfer head pattern to square, using a sharp pencil. Machine-stitch along the outline; trim away excess fabric, leaving ⅛″ seam allowance. Carefully make a slit in center of head, cutting through only one thickness of fabric. Turn head through slit; stuff firmly and hand-stitch slit closed. (Stitched side will be back of head.)

5. Using water-soluble marker, draw face on front of head. Color features with markers; lightly shade cheeks with the pink pencil.

6. For curly hair, make a bundle of small loops by winding yarn around two

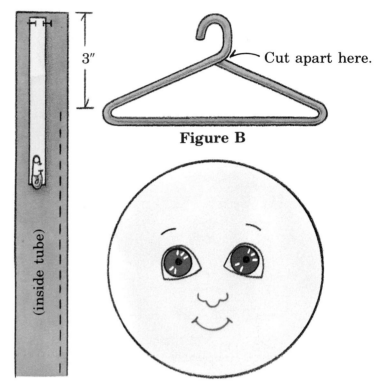

Figure A **Face Pattern**

3″

(inside tube)

Cut apart here.

Figure B

fingers six times; tie bundle in center with yarn. Make four more bundles. Fan out loops and glue bundle centers across top of the head, from "ear to ear." Tie a bow with narrow ribbon and glue to hair. Let the glue dry.

For pigtails, make a bundle of large loops by winding yarn around your hand 15 times; tie bundle in center with yarn. Using matching thread, hand-stitch loops through center to top of head. Smooth one side of loops against side of head and tack securely about halfway down; repeat for other side. Tie bows with narrow ribbon and glue on top of pigtail stitching. Make a bundle of small loops (as for curly hair) and glue to head for bangs.

7. Glue piece of eyelet to back of head, forming a collar. Sew button to chin; tie a bow and glue just above the button. Glue back of head to hanger, using generous amount of glue. Let dry.

Wooden Plane

Wood scraps, a handful of screws, and a few basic tools are just about all a woodworker needs to prepare this plane for takeoff. Fueled with imagination, it'll be flying high in the sky as soon as it's discovered under the tree.

You will need:
Tracing paper
Carbon paper
1 (18″-long) 2 x 4
3′ piece of Hollywood base
1 (6″-long) 1 x 4
3″ piece of molding (about ¼″-thick and
  ½″-wide) for propeller
Electric saber saw
Electric drill
Keyhole saw attachment (with ¼″ shaft
  and 1¾″ saw)
Sandpaper
5/16″, 7/64″, and 5/32″ drill bits
Countersink bit
4 (1½″) #10 oval-head wood screws
White glue
3″ (¼″-diameter) wooden dowel
1 (1½″) #6 round-head wood screw
Paintbrushes and acrylic paint (optional)

1. Trace patterns for body, front and
back wings, and tail on tracing paper.
Using carbon paper, transfer patterns to
wood as marked. Cut out pieces, using the
saber saw. Using drill and saw attachment, cut two wheels from the 1 x 4.

2. Using sandpaper, round off ends of
molding for propeller. Sand cut edges of
all pieces smooth.

3. Drill axle hole through body as
marked, using drill and 5/16″ bit.

4. Using drill and countersink bit, drill
two countersink holes in center top of
front wings as marked. Center the front
wings on the body. Using drill and 7/64″
bit, drill a hole through wings and into
body, at each countersink hole. Secure
front wings to body with two oval-head
wood screws.

5. Using drill and countersink bit, center and drill two countersink holes in underside of body as marked. Glue back wing to body and glue tail to back wing. When glue is dry, turn plane over. Using drill and 7/64″ bit, drill a hole through wing and into tail, at each countersink hole. Secure wing and tail with two oval-head wood screws.

6. Put glue on one end of dowel and insert through hole on one wheel. Insert other end of dowel through axle hole in body; glue remaining wheel onto end. Let the glue dry.

7. Using drill and 7/64″ bit, center and drill a hole in nose of body as marked. Using 5/32″ bit, drill a hole through center of propeller. Mount propeller with round-head wood screw, allowing room for propeller to turn freely.

8. Paint plane, if desired, and let dry.

countersink hole placement

Place on fold.

Front Wing
Cut one from Hollywood base.

Place on fold.

Back Wing
Cut 1 from
Hollywood base.

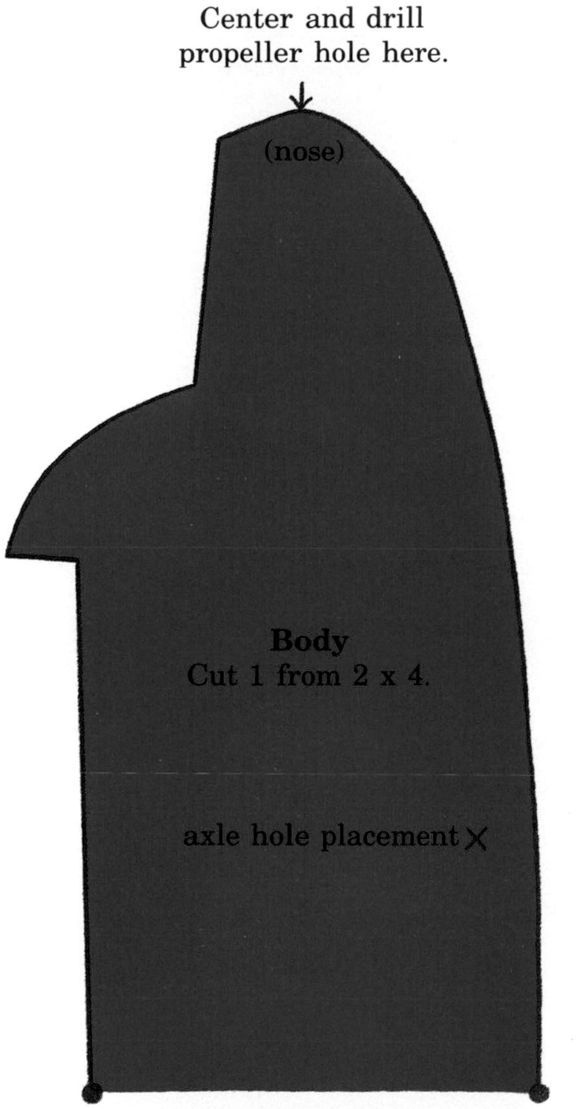

Center and drill
propeller hole here.

(nose)

Body
Cut 1 from 2 x 4.

axle hole placement ✕

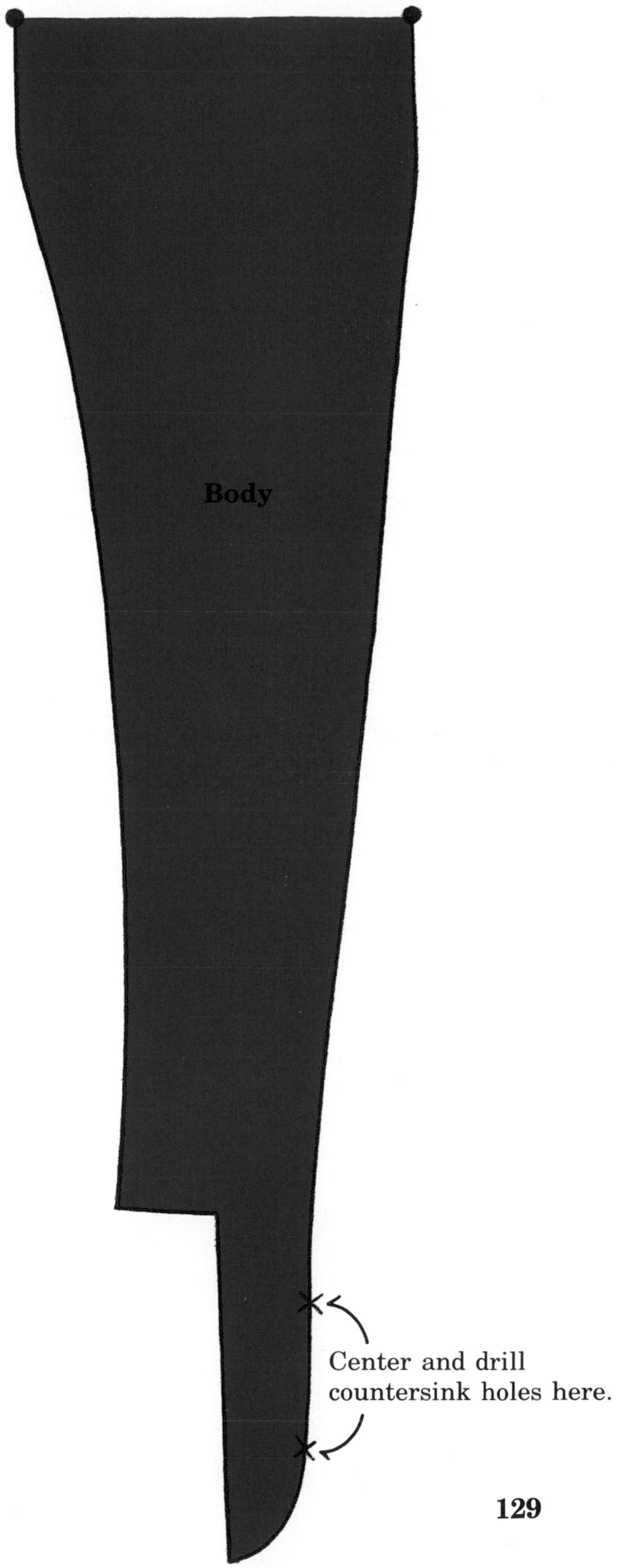

**For body pattern, trace one
complete pattern, matching dots.**

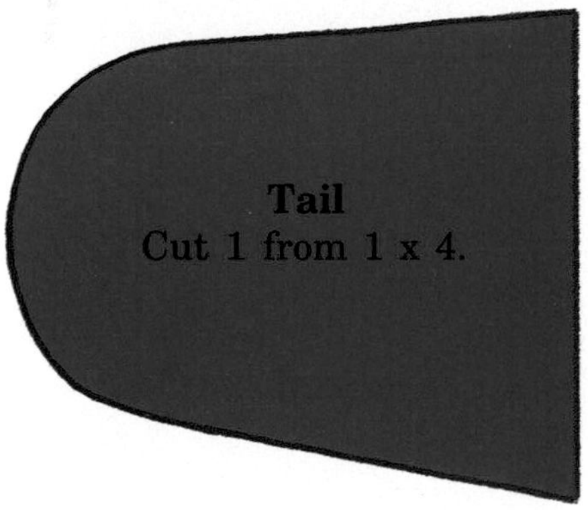

Tail
Cut 1 from 1 x 4.

Body

Center and drill
countersink holes here.

129

Missy Mouse Pajama Bag

An adorable mouse to have in the house, this one has a pocket and a penchant for pjs!

You will need:

1 yard (45″-wide) pink print fabric (head, outer ears, pocket, sleeves, bloomers)

1 yard (45″-wide) pink-and-white striped fabric (inner ears, arms, legs, tummy, body, tail)

⅓ yard (45″-wide) turquoise dotted fabric (cheek, nose, trim for sleeves and bloomers)

⅓ yard (45″-wide) turquoise print fabric (bow)

Thread to match

1 yard (45″-wide) fleece

Polyester stuffing

½ yard (¼″-wide) elastic

⅛ yard fusible web

Embroidery needle

Green embroidery floss

Black shank-button for eye

1 yard (1/16″-widc) pink ribbon

11″ (1¼″-wide) elastic

Wire clothes hanger (heavy gauge but bendable)

3 (⅝″-diameter) snaps

1⅓ yards (⅝″-wide) yellow polka-dot ribbon

1 yard (⅜″-wide) yellow ribbon

1 yard (1″-wide) yellow ribbon

Cutting the Pieces

1. Transfer patterns for head, outer ears, inner ears, cheek, nose, arms, and legs and cut as marked.

2. From pink print fabric, cut one 24½″ x 27″ rectangle (pocket) and four 6″ x 10″ rectangles (sleeves and bloomers). From striped fabric, cut one 9½″-diameter circle (tummy), one 2″ x 18″ strip (tail), and two 16″-diameter circles (body front and body back). Cut four 3¼″ x 10″ strips (trim for sleeves and bloomers) from dotted fabric and one 11″ x 45″ strip (bow) from turquoise print fabric. From fleece, cut one 9½″-diameter tummy circle and one 16″-diameter body circle.

Figure A

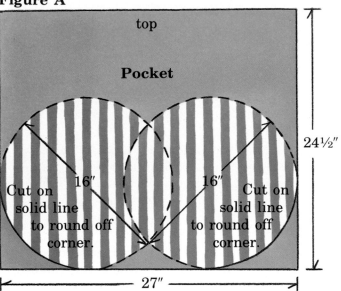

3. Using a 16″ circle, round off bottom corners of pocket rectangle. (Figure A.)

Note: Use ¼″ seam allowances throughout project unless instructed otherwise.

Making the Bag

1. For each arm and leg, sew two pieces, right sides together, leaving top open. Clip curves; turn piece right side out and stuff firmly to within ½″ of opening.

2. Cut the ¼″ elastic into four 4½″ lengths. To make each sleeve and bloomer, stitch 10″ edge of one pink print rectangle to 10″ edge of turquoise dotted rectangle, right sides together. Press seam toward turquoise.

Press remaining 10″ turquoise edge ¼″ to wrong side. Fold turquoise, 1″ from seam, to wrong side of pink (Figure B).

Figure B

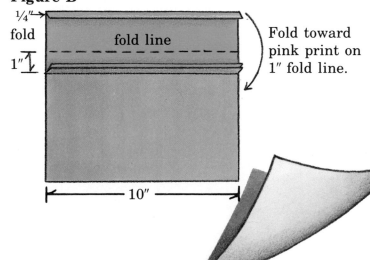

Press. Lay one piece of elastic along ¼" turquoise fold; zigzag elastic through all thicknesses, stretching it as you sew, to fit 10" piece.

Run a row of gathering stitches across 10" raw edge of sleeve (bloomer), beginning and ending ¼" from sides. With right sides together, sew side edges. Turn piece and press, with seam centered.

3. Slide sleeves and bloomers onto stuffed arms and legs, placing seams at center back. Gather raw edges of sleeves and bloomers; machine-baste gathered edges around raw edges of arms and legs.

4. Fuse cheek and nose to head front. Using matching thread and satin stitch, machine-appliqué the pieces. Embroider the mouth, using three strands of green floss and outline stitch.

Baste a fleece head to wrong side of each fabric head. With right sides of fabric heads together, stitch head, leaving neck open. Trim fleece and clip curves. Turn head and press; stuff lightly.

5. Fuse inner ears to two outer ears. Using pink thread, appliqué inner ears. Baste a fleece ear to wrong side of each appliquéd ear. With right sides together, stitch appliquéd ears to plain ears, leaving straight edges open. Clip curves; turn and press ears.

Turn raw edges of ears ¼" to the inside and blindstitch openings closed. Pleat ear for front of head as shown (Figure C); reverse pleat for remaining ear. Blindstitch ears to head, referring to Figure D for placement.

Figure C

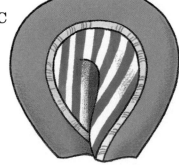

6. Sew button eye in place. To make whiskers, cut pink ribbon into 5", 6", and 9" lengths; knot middle and ends of each piece. Using matching thread, tack center knots of whiskers to head, referring to pattern for placement.

7. For tail, fold striped strip in half lengthwise (long edges together), with right sides together. Sew across one end and down long edge, leaving remaining end open. Clip corner; turn tail and stuff firmly to within 1" of opening.

8. To form casing, fold top edge of pocket piece ¼" and then 1½" to wrong side; press. Stitch, sewing close to the ¼" fold.

Baste fleece tummy circle to wrong side of striped tummy circle. Using matching thread, appliqué tummy (fleece side down) to center of pocket piece, 4" from top edge.

Thread the 1¼"-wide elastic through casing; baste ends of elastic to ends of casing. Run a gathering stitch down one side of pocket piece, across bottom, and up other side, stitching ¼" from edges.

9. Pin raw edge of head (face down) to right side of body front circle at center top; stitch. Flip head up. Position pocket (right side up) on right side of body front. Gather sides and bottom of pocket to fit body front; pin and baste, leaving neck open.

Pin arms (sleeve seams down) to body front/pocket, 3" from neck; pin legs (bloomer seams up) ¾" from center bottom; and pin tail 3" from leg. (Figure D.) Stack the following pieces, in order given: 16" fleece circle, body front/pocket (right side up), body back circle (right side down). Stitch all around through all layers, using ½" seam allowance and leaving neck open; stitch again, ¼" from first line of stitching, to reinforce. Reach hand through neck opening, between pocket

Figure D

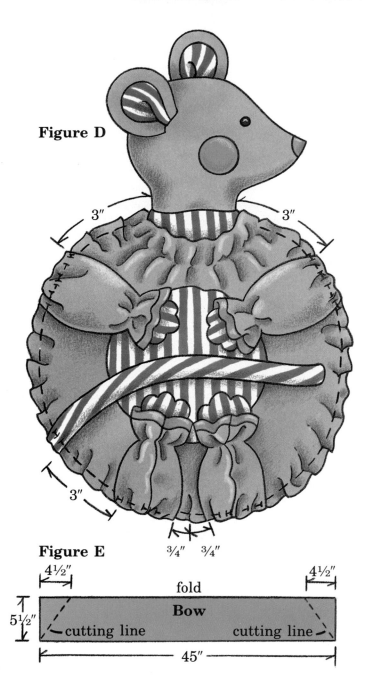

3" 3"

3"

Figure E

¾" ¾"

4½" 4½"

fold

Bow

5½"

cutting line cutting line

45"

and body back, and turn bag right side out.

Finishing the Bag

1. Bend hanger to conform to shoulder curves. Slide hanger into neck opening, leaving hook exposed; blindstitch opening closed. Tack hook securely to back of head. Tie three 1″ loops (for hanging) with the ¹⁄₁₆″-wide ribbon; tack loops to back of the bag, at top of arms and bottom of back ear.

2. For pocket closure, sew three snaps to neck and casing.

3. Fold bow strip in half lengthwise, with right sides together; cut ends at angle as shown. (Figure E.) Stitch across one end, down long raw edges, and across remaining end, leaving 4″ opening in long edge for turning. Clip corners; turn piece and press. Blindstitch opening closed. Tie bow and securely tack center to center front of pocket casing.

4. Cut the ⅝″ yellow polka-dot ribbon in half and tie into bows around zigzagging on bloomers. Cut two 15″ lengths of ⅜″ yellow ribbon; tie into bows around zigzagging on sleeves. Tie the 1″ yellow ribbon into a bow around end of tail.

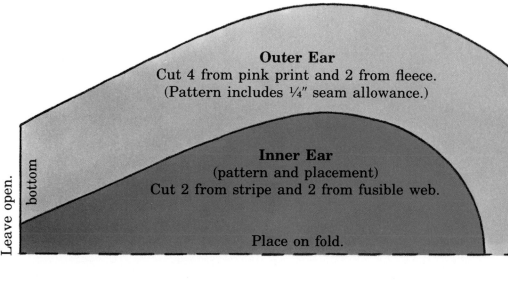

Leave open.

bottom

Outer Ear
Cut 4 from pink print and 2 from fleece.
(Pattern includes ¼″ seam allowance.)

Inner Ear
(pattern and placement)
Cut 2 from stripe and 2 from fusible web.

Place on fold.

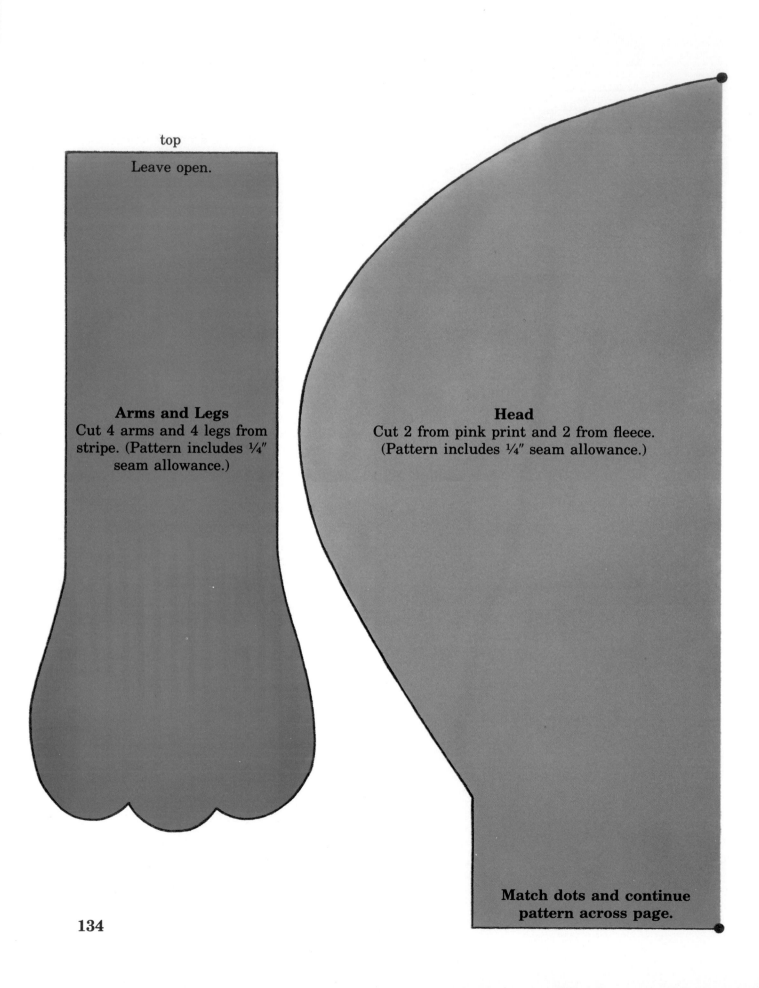

top

Leave open.

Arms and Legs
Cut 4 arms and 4 legs from stripe. (Pattern includes ¼″ seam allowance.)

Head
Cut 2 from pink print and 2 from fleece. (Pattern includes ¼″ seam allowance.)

Match dots and continue pattern across page.

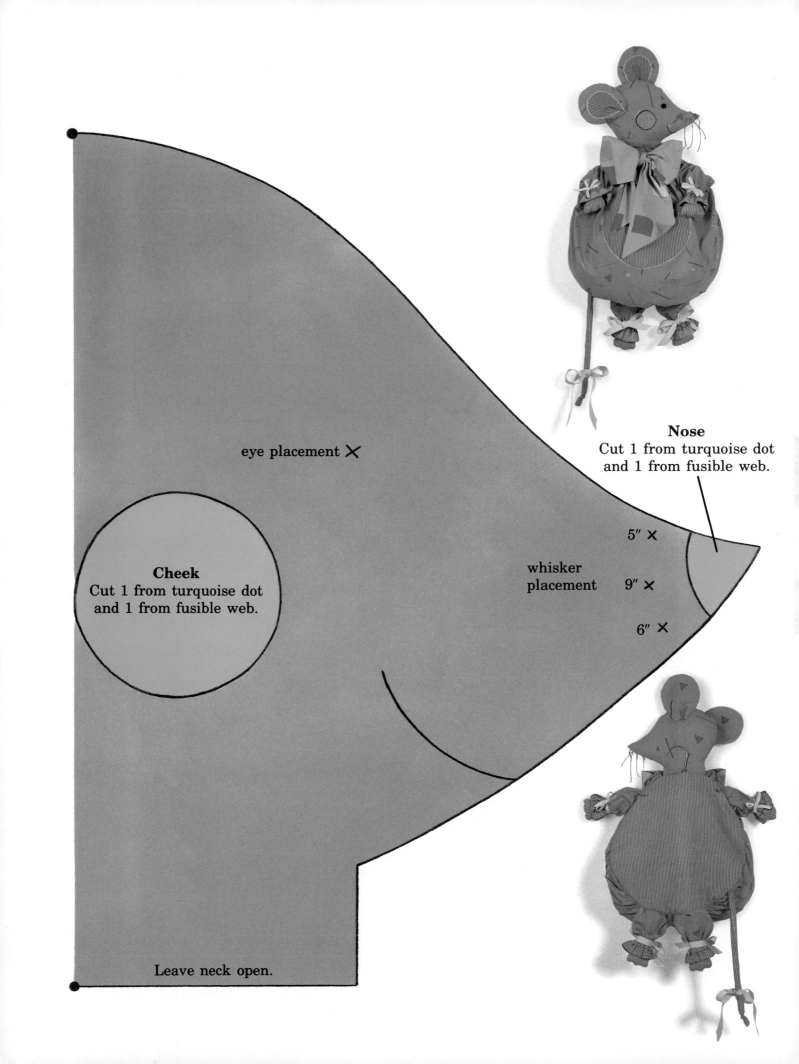

eye placement ✕

Cheek
Cut 1 from turquoise dot
and 1 from fusible web.

Nose
Cut 1 from turquoise dot
and 1 from fusible web.

5" ✕

whisker
placement   9" ✕

6" ✕

Leave neck open.

Jungle Tent

For youngsters, a tent is a ticket to hours of imaginative play. Pitch this one, and before you know it, a thrilling safari will be under way.

Although time-consuming, sewing this tent is not difficult, and shortcuts can be taken. For example, the multi-colored strips (which do a beautiful job of pulling the tent colors together) are pieced from solid-colored strips. Substitute striped strips or a variety of solid-colored ones for these, and you'll finish faster—and still have a tent with plenty of zip!

You will need:
1¾ yards (45″-wide) white cotton fabric
4½ yards (45″-wide) red cotton fabric
⅓ yard each light blue, dark blue, yellow, and green (45″-wide) cotton fabrics
Water-soluble fabric marker
Stencil plastic
Craft knife
Masking tape

Fabric paint (green, red, yellow, brown, light blue, and white)
Stencil brushes
Fine-tip paintbrush
Black fine-tip pen (permanent)
4 (¾″) 10-foot lengths PVC pipe
2 (¾″) 3-way PVC joints
4 (¾″) PVC elbows
Hacksaw

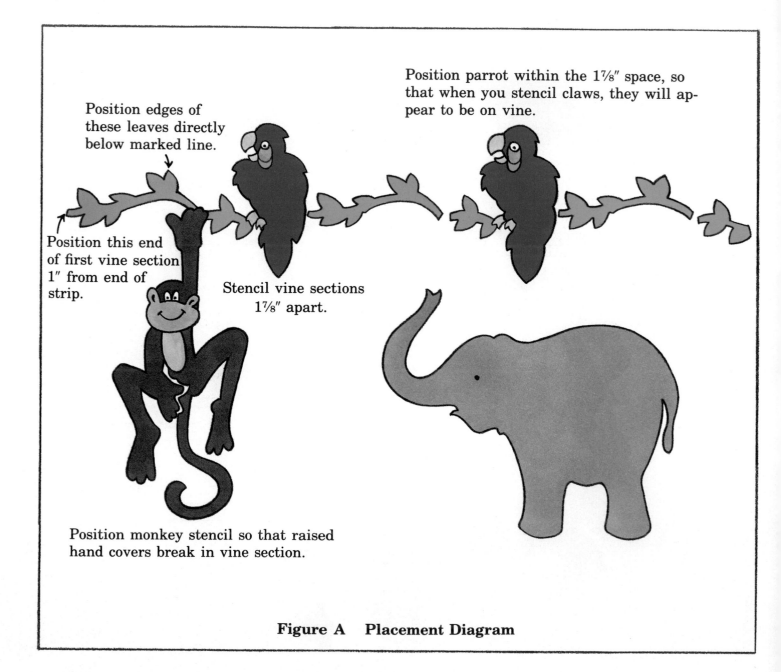

Position edges of these leaves directly below marked line.

Position parrot within the 1⅞″ space, so that when you stencil claws, they will appear to be on vine.

Position this end of first vine section 1″ from end of strip.

Stencil vine sections 1⅞″ apart.

Position monkey stencil so that raised hand covers break in vine section.

Figure A   Placement Diagram

Note: Launder fabrics before cutting.

Stenciling

1. Cut two 19½″ x 56″ strips from white fabric. On each strip, use the fabric marker to draw a line the length of the strip, 4½″ from top long edge. Label each strip #1.

2. Transfer stencil patterns to plastic. Cut out stencils, using the craft knife.

3. Position vine section stencil on one strip as shown (Figure A) and secure with masking tape. Using green paint and a stencil brush, stencil first vine section. Continue stenciling vine sections across the strip, leaving 1⅞″ between sections. (Figure A.) Repeat for remaining strip.

4. On each strip, use red paint to stencil a parrot body at end of each vine section, within the 1⅞″ space, as shown. (Figure A.) Stencil parrot beaks and claws yellow. (Figure A.) Using the paintbrush, paint green and light blue sections of parrot eyes. (Figure B.)

Figure B

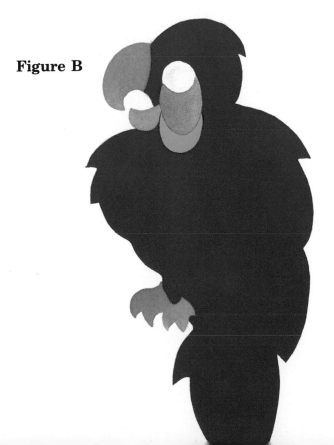

Figure C

5. On each strip, stencil a brown monkey body to left of first parrot as shown. (Figure A.) Stencil second monkey body between third and fourth parrot; stencil third monkey body between sixth and seventh parrot.

6. On each strip, stencil an elephant between first and center monkey, using light blue paint. (Figure A.) Stencil second elephant between center and last monkey.

7. To make tan paint for monkey face and chest, mix very small amount of brown with white paint. Stencil face and chest on each monkey.

8. When paint is thoroughly dry, use the black pen to outline beaks, claws, and eyes on parrots; draw pupils. Dot eyes on elephants. (Figure A.) On each monkey, outline face and eyes; draw pupils, mouth, and ears. (Figure C.)

Figure D

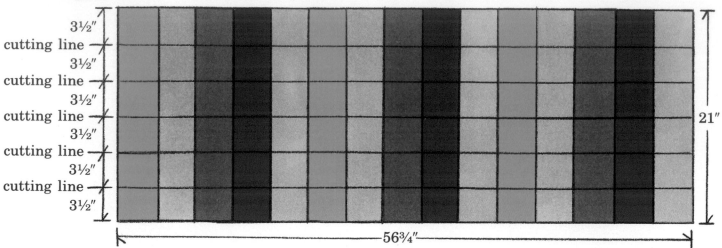

3½"
cutting line
3½"
cutting line
3½"
cutting line
3½"
cutting line
3½"
cutting line
3½"

21"

←————————56¾"————————→

Sewing the Tent

Note: Use ¼" seam allowances throughout project.

1. From each of the following fabrics, cut three 4¼" x 21" strips: light blue, red, dark blue, yellow, and green. With long edges and right sides together, sew the fifteen strips to form a multi-colored block of strips (approximately 21" x 56¾") as shown. (Figure D.) Cut block horizontally into six 3½" x 56¾" strips. (Figure D.) Label each of these strips #2.

2. From red fabric, cut two 5" x 56" strips (#3) and two 15¼" x 56" strips (#4). Label strips as indicated.

3. With right sides and long edges together, stitch strips as shown (Figure E) to form tent.

4. For tent pole casings, cut two 7" x 56" strips (#5) and four 7" x 45" strips (#6) from red fabric. Label as indicated.

5. To sew casing strips, turn all raw edges ¼" to wrong side and press; stitch ends (short edges) only. Fold strips in half lengthwise, wrong sides together, and press. With raw edges of tent between folded raw edges of strips, stitch casings to tent, positioning them as shown. (Figure F.) Turn under ends of center multi-colored strips and stitch.

140

6. For tent braces, cut two 2½" x 67" strips from red fabric. Turn raw edges on strips ¼" to wrong side and press. Fold strip in half lengthwise and stitch. At either end of strips, make a 3" loop; stitch. (See Figure G. When assembling the tent, you will slip these braces onto the A pipes to prevent the B pipes from sliding apart.)

Assembling the Tent

1. From PVC pipe, cut the following and label as indicated: two 58⅜" lengths (A), four 46½" lengths (B), and one 56" length (C). Label the two 3-way joints (D) and the four elbows (E).

2. With assistance, assemble tent frame as shown. (Figure G.) On one side of frame, take A, E, and B apart, at front and back. Slip a pair of #6 casings onto Bs; rejoin Es and Bs. Slip a tent brace (one looped end) onto A, then #5 casing and remaining tent brace. Rejoin A to Es. Repeat for other side of frame.

Figure G

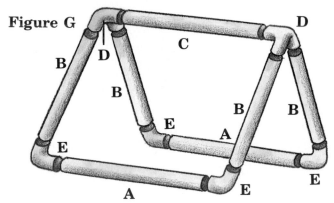

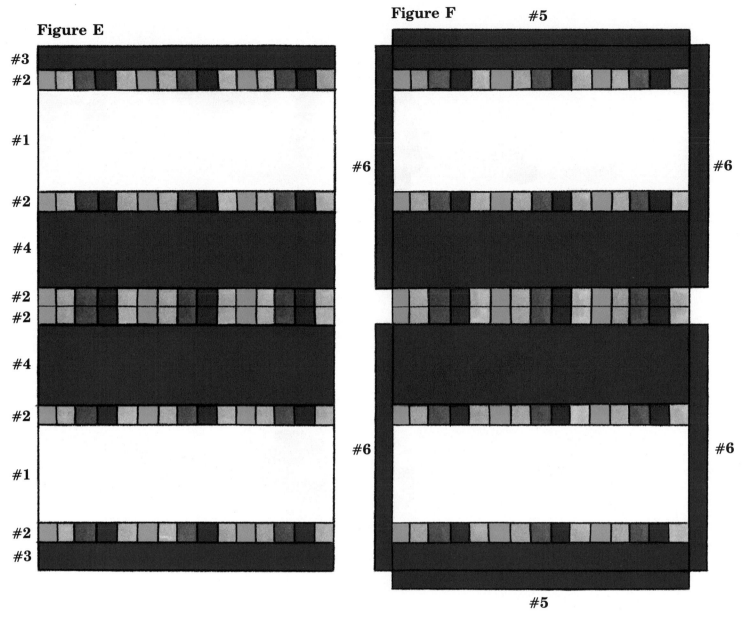

Figure E

#3
#2
#1
#2
#4
#2
#2
#4
#2
#1
#2
#3

Figure F

#5
#6
#6
#6
#6
#5

Vine Section

Parrot Body

Monkey Body

**Parrot Beak
and Claws**

142

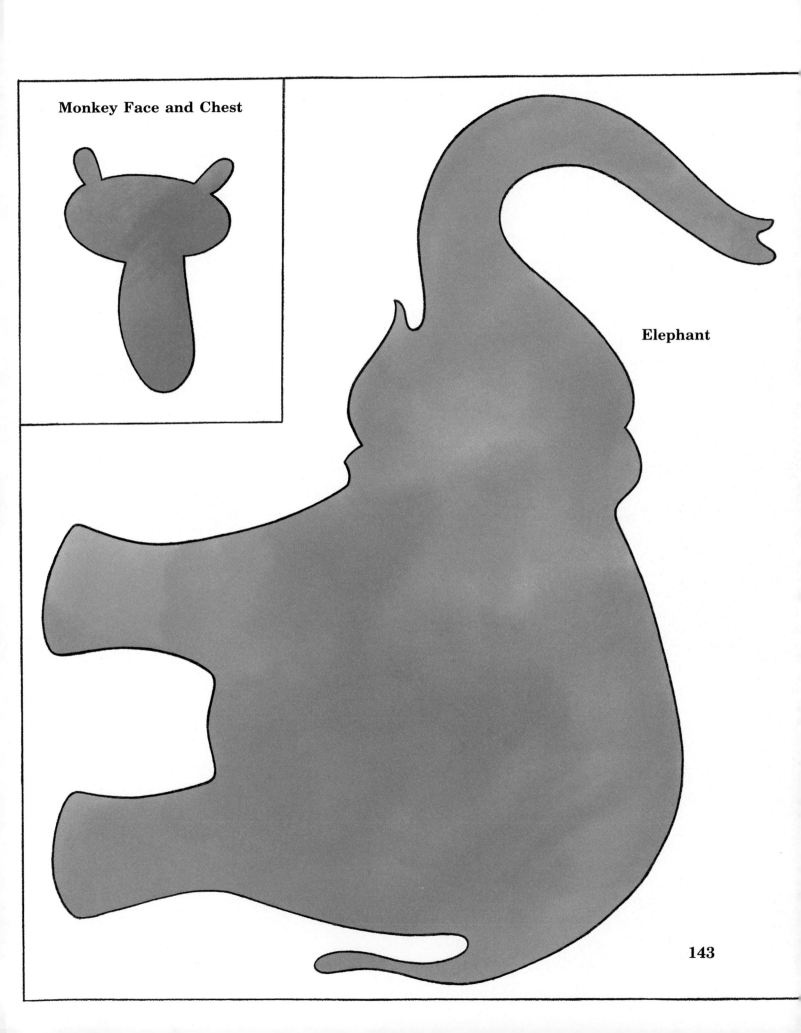

Monkey Face and Chest

Elephant

143

Designers & Contributors

Marina Anderson, Pocket Pony Sweat-suit, 86; Teddy Peg Rack, 112; Honey Bunny, 116.

Amy Albert Bloom, Shoe-Box Train, 36; Reindeer Wrap, 48.

Chere Brodsky, Cookie-Cutter Kids, 24; Cowboy Pete, 54.

Connie Formby, Window Wonderland, 38; Sponge Wrap, 46; Santa Claus Paper-dolls, 57.

Joyce M. Gillis, Hand-Painted Pot-holders, 64; Sugarplum Fairy Wand, 100.

Miriam C. Gourley, Jungle Tent, 136.

Barb Griffin, Chris-Mouse Sleep Set, 74; Vest-Dressed, 92; Dear Dolly Hangers, 124.

Linda Hendrickson, Peppermint Ponies, 22; Jumping Jack, 28; Cheery Trio, 30; A Colorful Crèche, 40; Nifty Necklaces, 62; Stenciled Garden Gear, 66; Pet Stockings, 68; Santa Puzzle, 98; Kangaroo Camp Kit, 106; Crocodile Crunch, 120; Missy Mouse Pajama Bag, 130.

Gerry Morris for S.G. Morris Designers, Cow Sweater, 77.

Walter M. Rush, Jr., Wooden Plane, 126.

Kathleen A. Taylor, Blue-Ribbon Bibs, 80; Goodnight, Barrettes, 103.

Carol M. Tipton, Nisse Dolls, 11; Friendship Star, 15; Star Piñata, 13; Paper Plate Angel, 33.

Wilma Wallace, Handy-Dandy Door Decoration, 44.

Madeline O'Brien White, Santa Cones, 26.

Linda Baltzell Wright, Patchwork Cards, 51.

Special thanks to the following shops in Birmingham, Alabama, for sharing their resources: **The All-American Kid; Applause Dancewear & Accessories; Chocolate Soup, Inc.; Ed's Pet World; Huffstutler's Hardware Home Center; Jack N' Jill Shop; Kiddieland Shop; Little Hardware; New Environs, Inc.; Petit Mom & Co.; Playfair, Inc.; Sikes Children's Shoes; Smith's Variety of Mountain Brook; Vestavia Hills Apothecary.**